IMAGES
of America

WASHINGTON COUNTY
UNDERGROUND
RAILROAD

IMAGES
of America

WASHINGTON COUNTY UNDERGROUND RAILROAD

Henry Robert Burke and Charles Hart Fogle

ARCADIA

Published by Arcadia Publishing,
an imprint of Tempus Publishing, Inc.
Charleston SC, Chicago, Portsmouth NH,
San Francisco

Printed in Great Britain.

Library of Congress Catalog Card Number: 2004100696

For all general information contact Arcadia Publishing at:
Telephone 843-853-2070
Fax 843-853-0044
E-Mail sales@arcadiapublishing.com
For customer service and orders:
Toll-Free 1-888-313-2665

Visit us on the internet at http://www.arcadiapublishing.com

(*Cover*) Ed Curtis drives a wagon down the Underground Railroad route between Markey and Stafford Stations. This rural route remains unchanged today. The wagon was either the original wagon used to transport fugitive slaves escaping to freedom, or it was the identical replacement built by the owner to replace the original when it became to dilapidated to make the trip.

CONTENTS

ACKNOWLEDGMENTS

A lot of credit should go to the people and institutions who shared their knowledge to make this book possible. These include but are not limited to the following:

Anna Curtis Burke, the Washington County Public Library, the Wheeling Public Library, Traci Booth McKitrick, the Washington County Historical Society, the town of Mount Pleasant, the Campus Martius Museum, the Belpre Historical Society, the Marietta College Library, Michael Perdreau, Ray Swick, Louise Zimmer, Dr. Richard Walker, Scott Britton, Lila Hull, Nancy Hoy, Ernie Thoad, Rachal Sipe, Jerry Devol, Burt Devol, Ben Bain, Kathy Lahotsky, Charlie Miracle, Rodger Patterson, John Briley, Mary Alice Casey, Al and Aida Adams, Joe and Enid Burke, Burdett Dalton, Cathie Nelson, Ed Curtis, John Curtis, Sheryl Corp, Lester Feltner, Michael Ralston , Sandra Moats, Frank Troutman, Dick Thomas, the Delong family, Clyde Mayle, Anna Henry, the Lawton family, Gaylor Layton, Howard and Molley Varner, Gerald and Grace Vance, Fran and Ruth Thornly, Joanne Smith Alexander, Gertrude Wilson, Dave Grande, Cora Wooten Rush, Gertrude Curtis Wilson, Bertha Lee Brown, the Wood County Public Library, the University of West Virginia at Morgantown, Hope Alison Woods, Dan and Nita Hinton, Rodger Young, Gary Wallace, and Vanessa Jay.

INTRODUCTION

This is a book about Southeastern Ohio and how it was involved in the Underground Railroad and the Abolition Movement between about 1760 and the First World War. As such, it is mostly a book about change. Slaves began trying to escape from bondage in the Ohio Country as soon as they began arriving in the mid to late 1700s. Most of those who tried found themselves trapped in a crown-canopied virgin forest where they lived in perpetual night even at midday. They could travel along rivers and streams, but there were no roadways. There were also Native Americans who knew the waterways and had hidden trails, but they often slaughtered escaped slaves as readily as they did their masters. And they practiced slavery themselves. Still some tried escaping, and some succeeded, depending on the isolation of the frontier to protect them from enforcers of fugitive slave laws.

But as settlers poured into the region, that isolation ended. The first recorded recapture of a slave who thought he had found freedom in the far off wilderness of Southeast Ohio occurred in 1804. Fugitive slaves who had crossed the Ohio River and found no place to hide on the Ohio side began showing up on the river bank in small towns like Belpre around 1808. People who thought slavery was wrong tried to help but they couldn't hide fugitives forever, and after 1797, helping them was against the law. Then in 1814 or 1815, the Underground Railroad was conceived and organized (mainly by veterans of the War of 1812) in Southeast Ohio. These veterans thought they could use contacts made during the war to move fugitive slaves north to freedom in Canada. It worked, but transportation was a nightmare. There were military roads built for earlier conflicts, but the war just passed. There were Indian trails. And there were short tracks to neighboring communities. But these were heavily traveled or guarded at key points.

So by and large in 1814, waterways were still the main routes for moving fugitives any distance in the heavily forested Ohio River Basin. The first escape routes for fugitive slaves were creeks and rivers. Stationhouses were the homes of the organizers.

Steamboats had appeared on the Ohio River in 1811, and their presence was enabling a new population explosion. But like the river itself, they were regulated by the South. Fugitive slave laws were enforced on their decks, and with the exception of a few packetboats with sympathetic owners, the Underground Railroad had to avoid them.

By the 1820s, expanding waves of Ohio settlers had begun connecting tracks and tying a simple road network together. In Southeast Ohio, this meant more freight and fugitives being moved overland, and the practice of using cover stories so fugitives could be moved by day began being practiced in some places. A second set of Underground Railroad Routes and Stations was established. This second set was located so as to take advantage of the new roads. People involved took to calling a bundle of routes and stations headed in one direction a "Line." Across the river in Virginia, at least two trans-Allegheny "turnpikes" appeared on maps.

These turnpikes made it easier to walk slaves west into the Ohio Country without crossing through Pennsylvania where slavery had been outlawed in 1780.

Also by the 1820s, the demand for slaves in the deep South had been so increased that the line of river-front slave auction blocks had grown into substantial businesses along the Ohio. They were located to take advantage of the growing network of steamboat transportation.

In the late 1820s and early 1830s, disguised Quakers began buying slaves at those auctions for the sole purpose of freeing them. Fugitive slaves were being guided along the new Virginia turnpikes at night by Underground Railroad conductors. In the 1830s, canal construction all across Ohio provided many new opportunities for fugitives to slip north as completed canals would a few years later. All along the canal paths, a third set of Underground Railroad stations was developed.

Sections of the new steam railroads came on line in the 1840s, and finally in the 1850s, there were trains across Southern Ohio connecting with the north/south escape routes of choice. These included both the Ohio and Erie Canal where it crossed the new steam rail line at Chillicothe and the eastern branch of the canal where it crossed the new rail line at Marietta. This meant a fourth set of stationhouses. It also meant that even after "North Western Virginia" was emptied of most of its slaves, a significant amount of Underground Railroad traffic used the Muskingum River Line.

In doing what they did, three generations of Underground Railroad people risked their lives repeatedly over 50 years. This book is an attempt to turn those 50 years into a series of snapshots in a context that shows what happened, while honoring the memory of those involved.

One
WATERWAYS

THE OHIO RIVER IN JANUARY (LOOKING EAST TO "OLD" VIRGINIA). In the early days of European settlement, the Ohio Valley was a forbidding place, a wilderness where total darkness pervaded even at noon in the crown canopied virgin forest. Streams and rivers were the only available routes for anyone trying to travel quickly. When a road system did begin to appear, it often had to be avoided by fugitive slaves who faced recapture and a return to very harsh treatment by their "owners." Under these circumstances, treacherous ice and black water could be seen as minor hazards. Streambeds that headed north away from the border were often preferred over turnpikes that did not.

DUCK CREEK LOOKING DOWNSTREAM. One such streambed was Duck Creek, shown here at a spot about three miles above its mouth on the Ohio River. Duck Creek tends toward waist deep waters with sand and smooth stones along its bottom. It is a pleasant place to be in the summer months. There has been at least a dirt track running along one bank or the other for almost 200 years due to early settlers who took trees along the banks for building tall ships for sale.

Duck Creek meanders north from the upriver edge of Marietta to Stafford by way of Stanleyville and Whipple and several other places—roughly 30 miles as the crow flies. And in the early 1800s (as those logged off patches became homesteads connected to each other by creek and road), the Duck Creek Route was a key component in the Underground Railroad. In later years, when other roads, canals, and finally railroads were built, escaping slaves would use only portions of the streambed routes. But in 1814, streams like Duck Creek were often the only options available for escaping the Ohio River border with Virginia and moving north through a dangerous wilderness.

DUCK CREEK LOOKING UPSTREAM.

BUCKLEY'S ISLAND. Seen here through the trees from the mouth of Duck Creek on the Ohio shore, Buckley's Island was used as a crossing point for freight during the day and escaping slaves at night. Actually, almost every Ohio River island served as a crossing point at one time or another. They were all legally part of the slaveholding states they bordered, but they shortened the crossing and were often unsettled and overgrown, and so provided dry ground with good cover where a party of fugitives might hide through the daylight hours.

ICE AT THE MOUTH OF DUCK CREEK IN FEBRUARY.

DUCK CREEK ROAD. The hills that show faintly in the background are in Old Virginia. The trees on the right are on the east bank of Duck Creek. The corn is in Ohio. For those who had arranged to meet their next conductor at Duck Creek's mouth, this old dirt road was a route on the Underground Railroad. At this location, the conductor was often Marietta's Stationmaster David Putnam Jr. or one of his agents. Duck Creek slid around Marietta's marshals and courts. It also avoided the late night boat crew carousers that populated the waterfront of the city proper all during the steamboat era. Duck Creek avoided all those hazards and lead fugitives to the Underground Railroad stations beyond.

LOWER END OF BUCKLEY'S ISLAND.

LITTLE MUSKINGUM RIVER. The Little Muskingum River empties into the Ohio River about two and a half miles upstream from the mouth of Duck Creek at a town called Reno. This was the beginning of the route used to move the slave woman Jane and her children towards Canada by way of Palmer, Markey, Stafford, and Collins Stations in southeast Ohio.

MUSKINGUM RIVER FOG. The photograph above was taken from a deck about 18 feet above water. Under these conditions, experienced local boatmen could often slip straight past the pursuit. Inexperienced boaters could end up lost until the fog cleared. The Muskingum River was always an important "line" on the Underground Railroad. But it reached its peak after 1841 when a canal expansion project connected the river by canal to Cleveland. Fugitives blended easily with the mobile canal crowd. The Muskingum segment of the canal never suffered the "southern" scrutiny that was always a problem on the southern end of the Portsmouth to Chillicothe segment completed in 1832.

BOATERS ON THE MUSKINGUM. Boaters at Marietta test a hand-built small boat of a design used in the 1800s.

"NEW" MOUTH OF GOOSE RUN. Most of it has been buried for more than a century now, but Goose Run still follows roughly the same course that it has since being rerouted as part of that canal expansion project. Even before it was rerouted, portions of it were used as an emergency route from its mouth on the Muskingum River to Marietta's emergency station at Eells House on land that is now part of Marietta College. The emergency station was needed because Marietta Stationmaster David Putnam Jr. and his stationhouse above Harmar Village were no longer secret. Putnam often debated and engaged in public brawls with pro-slavery types. By the mid-1830s, his place was staked out by pro-slavers who assumed he must be involved whenever slaves went missing. When it was not possible to go around this problem, there was Eells House.

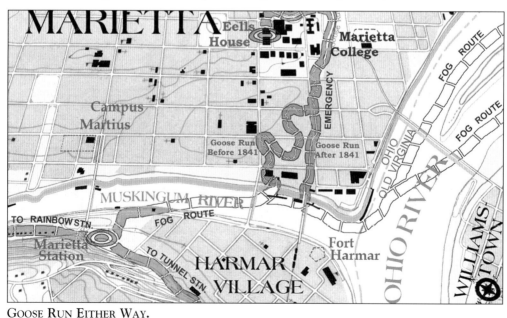

GOOSE RUN EITHER WAY.

LITTLE KANAWHA RIVER IN PARKERSBURG. Rivers on the Virginia side of the Ohio were also Underground Railroad routes. One key difference was that on the Little Kanawha (and the "big" Kanawha to the south) the upstream inventory of boats could be supplemented with barge loads of barrels, cut timber rafts, flatboats, floating trees, and anything else that would move downstream. Floating is quieter than rowing. It is easier to go unseen in a jumble of branches than on the deck of a boat. Once the Underground got organized, fugitives were not limited to jumbles. On the Little Kanawha in several documented instances, some of the barrels shipped on barges had fugitive slaves inside. According to Siebert, building hiding places into log rafts was standard practice for some lumbermen working the Kanawha River below Charleston. He also says that those rafts were crewed and met along the Ohio shore by Underground Railroad conductors.

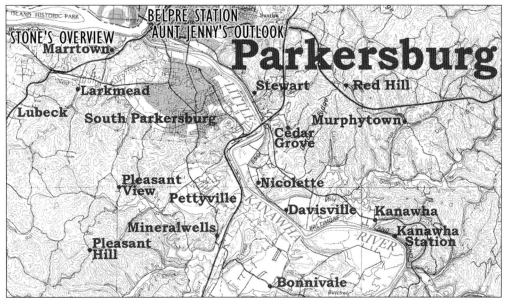

LITTLE KANAWHA RIVER A WAYS UPSTREAM.

LITTLE HOCKING RIVER. The Little Hocking, SR 555, and the Underground Route running north from Sawyer-Curtis Station all run up the same valley. In the beginning, of course the Little Hocking was the route. From Sawyer-Curtis Station below the river's mouth, fugitives went through Smith Station at Cutler and Hale and Bailey Stations near Bartlett to Quaker Inn Station at Chesterhill.

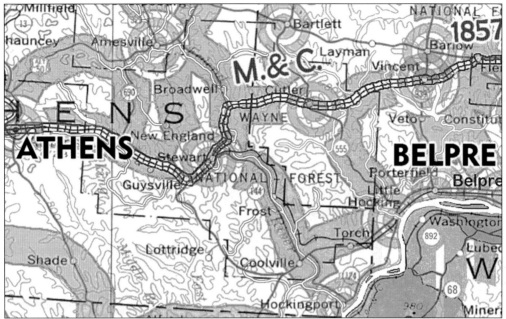

THE MARIETTA AND CINCINNATI RAILROAD. In the 1840s, the use made of both these rivers by the Underground Railroad was modified to meet changes in travel. The state had a new canal system. There were more roads, and then in the late 1840s and early 1850s, there were growing stretches of real rail lines. After 1857, it was possible to hop a train at Athens, Stewart, Cutler, or Vincent and ride to freedom.

HOCKING RIVER. The mouth of the Hocking River at Hockingport was a crossing station where Ohio-based conductors met parties of fugitive slaves needing to be guided upstream through Stewart Station and Brown Station at Aimesville. From there, in the early years, runaways were passed through a variety of stations funneling through Putnam Station at Zanesville.

SHADE RIVER. The Shade River (south of the Hocking) is perpetually shaded by the high sandstone ridge it cut through on its way to the Ohio. The Shade has no identifying sign where it passes under Ohio's coastal highway today, but because it cut through that ridge, it figured prominently in the early transportation routes in the Ohio Valley. The mouth of the Shade River was used as an Underground Railroad landing site, and in the early years, the river itself served as a route connecting to Hebbard's Station southwest of Athens.

RIVER BOATS. They were a part of the era. There were cases of small packet boat lines collaborating with the Underground Railroad to move fugitives north, but steam boats that worked the big rivers carried the South with them. Plantation owners and slave buyers rode them north to the auction blocks at Parkersburg, St. Marys, and Wheeling, and the slaves rode them back south. No slave or freed man was eager to make that trip.

THE OHIO RIVER. Seen from the heights behind Marietta's east side, the Ohio River assumes the look of the barrier it once was. The land pushing in from the right is Ohio. The river itself and the land on the far left were once Old Virginia. Before the Civil War, the river was part of the Mason-Dixon Line.

Two
ROUTES AND STATIONS

MARIETTA STATION (STATIONMASTER DAVID PUTNAM JR.). The David Putnam Jr. House was torn down in 1953 to make way for the new Washington Street Bridge across the Muskingum River. From here, Putnam sent his conductors south to meet parties of fugitives and bring them back across the river or to meet boatloads of runaway slaves on the Ohio shore. All through the 1830s and 1840s, this house was Marietta's main station on the Underground Railroad and that did become an open secret. In 1844, he smuggled two slaves out of his surrounded house disguised as one doctor in a hat and cloak. By 1847, when Putnam Jr. was named as a transporter of "stolen" slaves in a lawsuit filed by slave owner G.W. Henderson, crowds of pro-slavers had surrounded his house many times. Putnam, by all accounts an able stationmaster, was probably using himself as a diversion at that point in the endeavor.

HARMAR CEMETERY. This photograph of Harmar Cemetery where David Putnam Jr. is buried was taken through the trees from Fort Harmar Drive. Marietta's stationhouse stood between the camera and those stones.

MARIETTA TO RAINBOW STATION. Named for the creek that bordered the property on its downstream edge, Rainbow Station was the property of Stationmaster Thomas Ridgeway. The ferry Ridgeway operated made Rainbow Station an intersection point for several Underground Routes. Parties heading northeast through Middleburg or Stafford, north through Coal Run and Cambridge, or northwest through Putnam Station below Zanesville used that ferry. Some parties came from the west to cross at Rainbow. So some days, there was a two-way traffic of fugitives along the Muskingum River.

RAINBOW STATION (RIDGEWAY FARM). This photograph was taken from across the river *circa* 1880.

RAINBOW STATION NEIGHBOR. The white house in the distance in the middle was reclaimed by grapevines by 1997. This view is from the southwest.

POWER OF NATURE. It is very easy to disbelieve those descriptions of this area's virgin forests in the first chapter. The door on the left above is hidden under a crown canopy of grape vines that runs over the roof two stories above. This is a house, remember, that shone in the sunlight in the photograph of Rainbow Station 110 years before. The only reason you can see the door in this shot is that the photographer used a flash. The picture was taken around noon. The picture on the right above was taken without a flash. It is a view from under the edge of the canopy from the side porch. So those stories from the early days are true. Anyone with the courage to run off into those forests was brave and desperate.

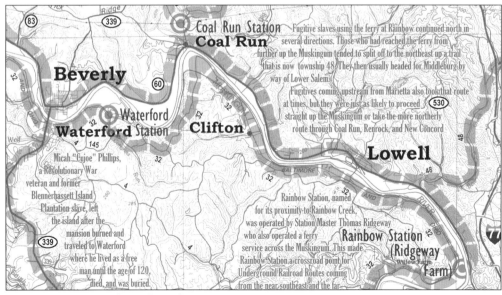

Coal Run Station — Fugitive slaves using the ferry at Rainbow continued north in several directions. Those who had reached the ferry from further up the Muskingum tended to split off to the northeast up a trail that is now township 48. They then usually headed for Middleburg by way of Lower Salem.

Fugitives coming upstream from Marietta also took that route at times, but they were just as likely to proceed straight up the Muskingum or take the more northerly route through Coal Run, Renrock, and New Concord.

Micah "Cujoe" Phillips, a Revolutionary War veteran and former Blennerhassett Island Plantation slave, left the island after the mansion burned and traveled to Waterford where he lived as a free man until the age of 120, died, and was buried.

Rainbow Station, named for its proximity to Rainbow Creek, was operated by Station Master Thomas Ridgeway who also operated a ferry service across the Muskingum. This made Rainbow Station a crossroad point for Underground Railroad Routes coming from the near southeast and the far

FROM RAINBOW TO COAL RUN STATION.

26

COAL RUN STATION. This is the Muskingum River as seen from Coal Run's turnoff, and 140 years after the fact, no one is quite sure which of the old farmsteads along the ridge behind us was the Coal Run Underground Railroad Station. Today, Coal Run isn't really visible from the state highway. So strangers seldom see it, but 140 years ago, Coal Run was at an important fork in the road. This made it an important place for people who needed to get to Crooked Tree or Ren Rock, and sometimes such people were fugitive slaves.

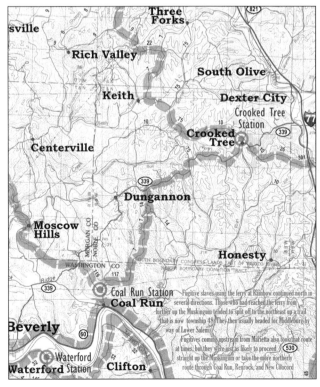

FROM COAL RUN TO CROOKED TREE STATION. Actually, fugitive slaves traveling up the Muskingum River from the county seat at Marietta often had more immediate reasons for wanting to leave the river at that point. From the top of the bluff at Coal Run, it is just under a mile to the tri-county line for Washington, Morgan, and Noble counties. In the 1830s (and possibly other decades as well), the local sheriff, Washington County's Sheriff, was a southern sympathizing, pro-slavery "Copperhead." This made crossing the county line an important act at times, and it made the establishment of an Underground Railroad Station near that county line with safe houses available in all three counties a very sensible move.

JUDGE EPHRIAM CUTLER. In 1806, Ephriam Cutler (left) settled where that gazebo-like structure pictured on your right now stands. He built a cabin, planted crops, and established a post office. Later he added a stone quarry. Here also, the first coordinated efforts of the clandestine network that would come to be known as the Underground Railroad took place sometime around 1814 or 1815. The people who met here to plan those efforts were mostly New Englanders by birth and veterans of the War of 1812. Their common heritage united them in opposition to slavery. Their wartime service had shown them the way to Canada and the free black population living there. They organized a chain of safehouses that ran from Ohio's eastern river counties to the Canadian shore of Lake Erie.

CONSTITUTION TO BARLOW STATION. Whatever the decade, fugitives arriving here had usually just crossed the Ohio by way of paths across Halfway or Neal Islands. Usually in the early years, the next stop was Barlow Station by the routes indicated on the map. In later years, fugitives moving through Judge Cutler's Station might be sent to Marietta by way of Tunnel Station to join a northerly moving canal work gang or to Vincent Station to meet a train. Ephriam Cutler was stationmaster here. Conductors working for him included Jules Demming and Dyar Burgesses.

CUTLER'S CONSTITUTION STATION. In the years that followed, many escaped slaves were guided to Constitution Station by underground conductors. Here, they were met by others who would take them away from the river and further up the line. Usually, they set out along a path that has since become CR 3 (seen stretching up the hill in the photograph above). At times, they moved secretly by night. At other times, they went openly by day, disguised as millstone delivery persons.

EPHRIAM CUTLER "VETOES" SLAVERY. Judge Cutler did not limit his antislavery efforts to those direct actions already described. The photograph above shows a plaque affixed to the front wall of the Ross County Courthouse at Chillicothe. On that spot in 1802, a very sick Ephriam Cutler was carried into the Statehouse pictured on the plaque by his fellow Washington County delegates Rufus Putnam and Paul Fearing. Once inside, he cast the vote that defeated a proposed amendment to the state constitution that would have made Ohio a slave state. The convention was almost evenly divided on the issue of slavery, and so, Ohio did miss becoming a slave state by one vote. Shortly after WWII, Veto Lake was created south of Barlow. The name commemorates the effect of Cutler's one vote—preventing slavery in Ohio.

ONE OF CUTLER'S MILLSTONES. Still at Constitution, this stone was not used as a prop in a fugitive's trip north like others were.

BARLOW STATION. Located just east of Barlow's town center, Barlow Station was built by Stationmaster James Lawton Sr. around 1819. In the early years, he received fugitives from Constitution Station to the south and Marietta to the east. He sent them on to Waterford in the north and Bartlett in the west. In later years, as has already been mentioned that would change. Lawton was also involved in the rescue of "Aunt Lacy," age 60. Aunt Lacy belonged to an old Virginian Free Mason. She was removed from his home along the river one day and taken 12 miles back into the interior as security for a debt. But she escaped her new captors and found her way back to his house, on foot, during a stormy night in late winter. For reasons unknown, her old master nursed her through the case of pneumonia that resulted and took her to some abolitionist Free Masons on the Ohio Side of the river. Aunt Lacy was not safe with them. So James Lawton moved her some 10 miles, traveling through a long night on a narrow untraveled road to do so. Some days later, after contact with a Mason in Harmar Village, Lawton was able to arrange for Aunt Lacy to be moved to Hills Landing below Little Hocking. There she was met by a theological student sent by her free son to take her back with him to Cincinnati, her son, and freedom.

HERROLD'S MILL STATION (ATHENS). In the early years, it was important that Herrold's Mill was located at the headwaters of the Hocking River, and at times, fugitives hid beneath the spillway. In the middle years, overland traffic was fed through Athens from a large group of Ohio landings all the way to down the mouth of the Kanawha River at Point Pleasant. From Athens, passengers tended to be sent north through Quaker Inn Station by way of Brown Station at Aimesville. From Quaker Inn at Chesterhill, traffic tended to move north along the Muskingum. In later days, the east/west steam rail line through Athens provided a lot of other options.

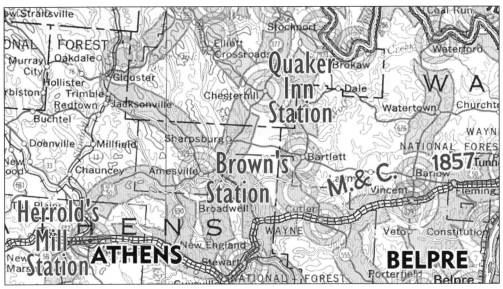

HERROLD'S MILL TO QUAKER INN STATION.

STATIONMASTER MICAJAH "CAJOE" PHILLIPS, WATERFORD STATION. Micajah "Cajoe" Phillips, now lies buried in a pasture near the spot where his home once stood. That home was Waterford Station. Located on what is now TR. 32 two miles east of Waterford on Constitution Run, Waterford Station was used by escaping slaves coming north along what is now SR 339 from Barlow Station. It was also used by those traveling up the Muskingum from Rainbow and Marietta Stations. Some fugitives left the river at Waterford and headed north by various routes. Others followed it northwest towards Zanesville. Phillips, born a slave, fought in the Revolutionary War under provision of a decree promising slaves who served a year or more their freedom, but after the war, he was returned to slavery. He was sold in the late 1790s to Harmon Blennerhassett, of Blennerhassett Island, and became a boatman there. Blennerhassett later

became involved in Aaron Burr's plot to found a separate empire in the west, and when the Blennerhassetts fled the island late in 1806, Phillips decided to free himself. He rowed to the Ohio shore and walked north, arriving at Waterford on the Muskingum early in 1807. There he stayed, establishing a farm and an Underground Railroad Station where he now lies.

NEW MARKER. This marker was added by a man who feared people would soon be unable to read the old headstone shrouded in weeds in the picture above.

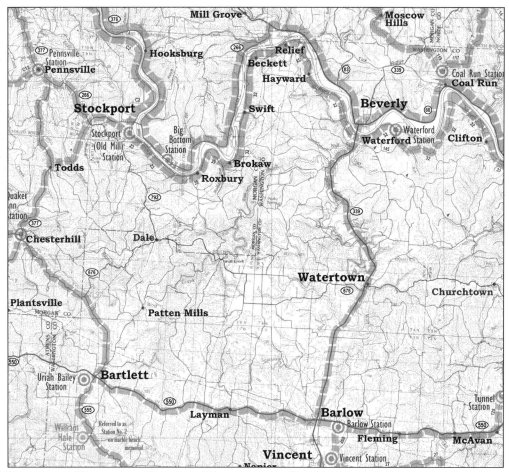

BARLOW TO WATERFORD STATION, WATERFORD TO BIG BOTTOM TO STOCKPORT STATION, AND BARLOW TO BARTLETT TO CHESTERHILL TO STOCKPORT STATION. Following the west bank of the Muskingum River, fugitives rode or walked about 15 miles to travel from Micajah Phillips' Waterford Station to the "Old Mill" Station at Stockport. Fugitives who crossed to the east bank and also headed upstream had the option of stopping at Big Bottom Station as well. Some Waterford parties moved downstream through Coal Run and then headed north, and of course, fugitives coming from Chesterhill or Pennsville and headed for Coal Run or Rainbow Stations might cover the same ground.

Many fugitives leaving Barlow Station headed west through Uriah Bailey Station at Bartlett and Quaker Inn Station at Chesterhill. Others went north, traveling at night along the unimproved dirt road that eventually would become SR 339. Those fugitives often sojourned at Micajah Phillips' Waterford Station when they reached the Muskingum.

BIG BOTTOM STATE PARK, STATION. Named for the broad Muskingum River Flood Plain that extends several miles downstream from Stockport and for the community that once stood here at its north end, this park was the site of an attack on the half-built Ohio Company settlement of Big Bottom. The attack was made by Shawnee, Delaware, Ottawa, Kakapo, and Wyandotte Braves under the command of Blue Jacket on Sunday January 2, 1791, and left 18 dead of 21. Despite warnings of hostile feelings against them and personal knowledge of Native American warfare, 21 of the 36 settlers were gathered in their uncompleted blockhouse without pickets or even a sentry when Blue Jacket's force descended on them. The Big Bottom Massacre, which resulted from that attack, left 18 dead with three survivors and marked the outbreak of four years of frontier warfare in Ohio.

Although it is gone now, the community of Big Bottom was resettled and completed after the massacre, and in later years, became an Underground Railroad Station and a center for abolitionist speakers. Large tents were set up with a speaker's platform and long rows of benches for public seating, and abolitionist seminars were held there in the style of the Chautauqua movement of the 1920s. People came from miles around. Of course, at a large gathering like that, it was hard to see who came or left with whom.

QUAKER INN STATION, CHESTER HILL. No picture or description of the Quaker Inn at Chester Hill has yet been found. What does remain at Chesterhill (one word now) is this old meeting house and the graveyard that stretches for some distance behind the photographer. It is certain that some of the people buried in this field served as agents, conductors, and stationmasters on the Underground Railroad, many through Quaker Inn Station. The Quaker Inn was part of the Underground Railroad from the founding of the Quaker community it served. The inn served non-Quakers as well. This lead more than once to an inn full of guests who were hunting for other people safely hidden on farms or in houses belonging to the staff that served them. Elias Bundy was stationmaster, and he operated from within a circle of "old and reliable friends" or "elders," as is the tradition for any important undertaking in a Quaker community. In that circle were Able W. Bye, Joseph Doudna, Jesse Hiat, Nathan Morris, Arnold Patterson, and Thomas K. Smith. A lot of "freight" came to Chesterhill from Bartlett Station, which was fed by stations ranging from Marietta to Parkersburg.

JOHN DOUDNA.

FRIENDS IN WINTER. As you can see from the sign above, this meetinghouse was not established until 1836. The Quaker Inn may have opened before that. Another stream of traffic reached Chesterhill from Athens area stations through Sharpsburg. Traffic leaving Chesterhill went to about seven different stations, but almost all of it ended up on the Muskingum Line by way of Zanesville. Quaker Inn Station was run quietly. Fugitives were hidden at farms nearby or at the mill at Stockport where the mill operator had the community believing he was pro-slavery. Residents of Chesterhill, meanwhile, could only note that one or more of the Quaker Elder Conductors was absent now and again.

STOCKPORT STATION (OLD MILL STATION). Grist mills, with their clouds of finely ground flour, were the early industrial equivalents of fuel air bombs. It is therefore no real surprise that the old mill at Stockport (recently remodeled into a spectacular bed and breakfast) is the third replacement structure for the old mill that originally served as Stockport's Underground Railroad safehouse. Actually, the Old Mill Station is also not in its old location, having started life some 300 yards downstream in 1841, but no matter. In 1841, the Muskingum River dam system (begun in 1836) started holding water at Stockport, the year the mill began to grind grain, and the year it first saw use as a refuge to fugitive slaves. According to W.H. Siebert, Stockport's mill operator maintained the fiction that he was a pro-slavery "Copperhead." He was thereby able to hide escapees in the mill itself and never be subjected to a search. The stationmaster at Stockport was not the mill operator, by the way. The stationmaster was Rial Cheadle, who rates his own page.

THE VIEW FROM THE MILL.

STATIONMASTER RIAL CHEADLE. According to Wilbur Henry Siebert, who began a lifelong project of interviewing Underground Railroad participants in 1891, Rial Cheadle was something special. In addition to serving as a conductor for stations spread from Putnam near Zanesville to Albany near Athens, Cheadle was an accomplished actor and used his talent for the cause.

When he lived at Stockport, he helped support the story that the mill owner there was a pro-slavery "copperhead." In reality, that worthy whose name has been lost in time was using the mill as Stockport's Underground Station safehouse. The actual stationmaster at Stockport was Cheadle, but no southern sympathizers suspected that was the case because Cheadle had them convinced that he couldn't walk and chew gum at the same time. He played the fool so well that no one he "played" for thought him capable of even looking after himself. When he lived in Ringold, his travels often took him deep into Old Virginia where he would pose as a "peddler of trinkets." Again, according to Siebert, "He was shrewd but acted as a witless man, and sang silly songs while abducting slaves from beyond the Ohio or leading them up the trail. Clandestine work at night was his principal occupation." According to Henry Burke, Cheadle was the motive force and idea man behind many of the strategies used to baffle fugitive slave hunters in his territory.

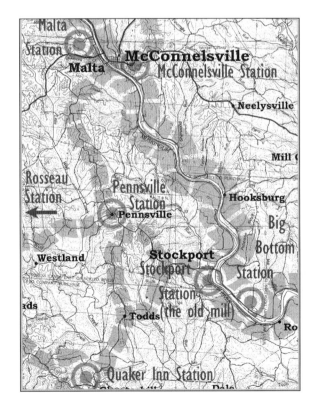

STOCKPORT TO MCCONNELSVILLE AND MALTA STATIONS.

MALTA/MCCONNELSVILLE. This picture was taken from McConnelsville. The house is in Malta. Both towns had stations, and from both towns, it was possible to watch packetboats pass by carrying fugitive slaves to freedom. But long before that, these towns were at the center of an Underground Railroad "X" made up of Stockport traffic headed for Deavertown and Pennsville traffic headed for Ren Rock.

GENERAL ROBERT MCCONNEL HOUSE. Former mayor and unofficial historian Gaylin Findly said he believes that fugitive slaves were given shelter in an outbuilding behind the house pictured below. It was the home of Revolutionary War General Robert McConnel, who founded McConnelsville in 1817. The general was an abolitionist. Today a row of new buildings block what must have been a fine view of the river when the house was built.

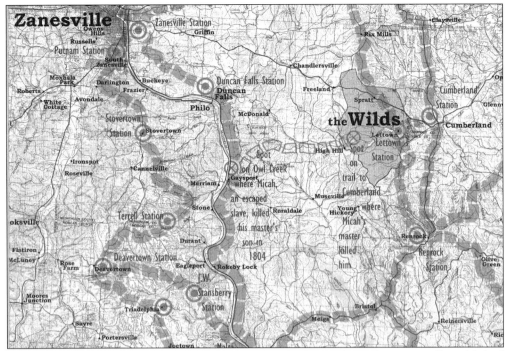

McConnelsville/Malta to Putnam Station. The routes shown here were all established in the teens the 1820s and 1830s. After 1841, the Muskingum itself and the new towpath alongside it got more traffic while the older routes got less.

Malta/McConnelsville Dam.

ROKEBY LOCK. Rokeby Lock is the nearest dam on the Muskingum to where Morgan's Raiders crossed the river on July 23 of 1863. They stole food and horses wherever they went but by then had quit "recapturing" people of color and sending them south.

DUNCAN FALLS LOCK AND DAM. Duncan Falls, Rokeby Lock, and other towns that did not get pictures here all sheltered fugitive slaves along the canal path from time to time, but like Malta, Duncan Falls was involved with the Underground Railroad before the "Improvement" and had a station.

PUTNAM'S CONSCIENCE. When the Underground Railroad and abolition movements reached their fullest roar in Ohio, the community of Putnam, known today as South Zanesville, was an abolitionist town while Zanesville had messy riots supporting the other side. In the 1840s, when the folks who went to the abolitionist lectures at Putnam United Presbyterian Church, built in 1835, they felt embattled.

PUTNAM'S STATION (THE STONE ACADEMY). First a would-be statehouse, then a place where Ohio's Anti-Slavery Society held conventions, the Stone Academy (located half way between the church and the river) was a private residence and Underground Railroad stationhouse after 1839.

PUTNAM LANDING. The ducks have taken over now, but Putnam Landing was busy back when the Stone Academy was built by speculators hoping to lure Ohio's Statehouse away from Chillicothe. It was still busy 30 years later when Putnam and Zanesville were on opposite sides in the national debate over slavery. At times, African Americans, fugitive and free, were warned to get off packet boats at Putnam rather than risk riding through Zanesville. Before the Muskingum was improved, Underground Railroad passengers came to Putnam by way of carriage and wagon rides from Duncan Falls on the east side of the river and through Deavertown Station by way of Terrell and Stovertown Stations on the west.

PUTNAM LANDING FROM THE EAST SIDE OF THE RIVER.

44

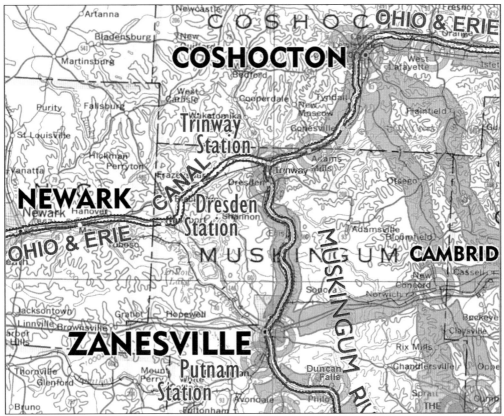

FROM PUTNAM TO TRINWAY STATION. From Stockport, the Muskingum River Line moved through seven stations before reaching the segment of the canal the Improvement Project connected with at Trinway. There was also a web of stations east and west of the river and a continuing series of stations along the canal from Chillicothe to Cleveland. There was a station at Coshocton that is now preserved as part of the Roscoe Village complex, but it is time to turn back to the Ohio River and pick up another thread of routes and stations

PUTNAM CHURCH SIGN.

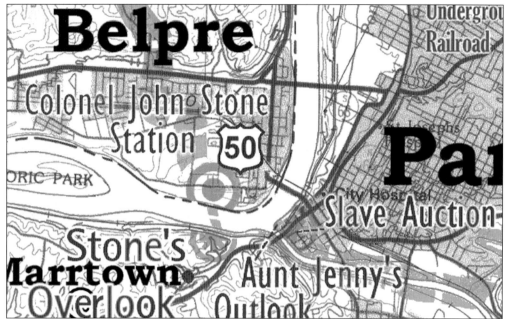

AUNT JENNY, COLONEL JOHN STONE, AND BELPRE STATION. The marker below stands in front of the house that was Stone's Station (at Belpre) on the Underground Railroad. As you can see from the map, it is located on Blennerhassett Avenue in Belpre where that road parallels the Ohio River from across Stone's Bottom. The marker honors Captain Jonathan Stone, the father of Colonel John Stone, who was a stationmaster on the Underground

Railroad. Captain Jonathan Stone built a three-family fort on the river bank due south of the marker in 1798. So Colonel Stone, like most adult residents of the region in the early 1800s, had practical experience gained from being raised during the last of the "Indian troubles" on a river well known for its pirates. The house behind the marker came later, but Stone's Bottom has been under continual cultivation for 200 years. When the fugitive slave laws were in effect, parties of fugitive slaves headed north occasionally hid behind the rows of corn there while waiting for a sheriff's patrol to pass or for their next Underground Railroad conductor to arrive. At other times, when the coast was clear, escaping slaves hid and rested in the stationhouse, in the safehouse next door, or in the barns beyond. Colonel John Stone, the stationmaster, was knowledgeable as to when it was safe because of the fine intelligence he had of slaver identities, plans, and intentions.

STONE'S BOTTOM WHERE FUGITIVES HID. The white house is Stone's Stationhouse. The Ohio River is hidden from this angle, but the hills on the far left are on the other side of it and used to be part of Virginia. Colonel Stone used a network of spies, observation posts, and signal lights. No slave was ever caught crossing the river at Belpre when the colonel said it was clear. Other slaves were recaptured at Belpre and tortured. Upstream at Marietta, Stationmaster David Putnam Jr. relied heavily on two black barbers, Jerry Jones and Daniel Strawther, who functioned very effectively as spies. They were all but invisible to the white men they clipped. At Belpre, Colonel Stone's most useful spy was a resident of the town across the river, a slave woman known as Aunt Jenny. Aunt Jenny was Parkersburg's "bell ringer" at the landing there. The bell ringer was charged with keeping track of boat arrivals 24 hours a day and by ringing a bell, notifying the slaves working the docks that it was time to start. A small shack on Parkersburg's point went with the job. So Aunt Jenny was trusted by her owners. She was also in the Underground Railroad, and she used her position to keep track of posse movements and preparations, which she then passed on to Colonel Stone in his white house and others in her organization.

STONE STATION, BELPRE.

SAWYER-CURTIS STATION (LITTLE HOCKING). Originally an inn on the old Chillicothe Pike out of Marietta, the structure now called Sawyer-Curtis House was built by Nathanial Sawyer in 1798. After passing through the hands of several owners, it was purchased by Horace Curtis in 1820. Curtis was a merchant, an abolitionist, and an Underground Railroad stationmaster. He established a successful general mercantile store next to the old inn, which he used as a home and as the Underground Railroad Station at Little Hocking. There was a hidden room in the basement that was used to hide fugitives. His was one of the few stationhouses actually overlooking the Ohio River, which at the time was part of the Mason-Dixon line and the earliest surviving building that became a stationhouse built in Ohio.

PLAQUE LOCATED BY BACK DOOR.

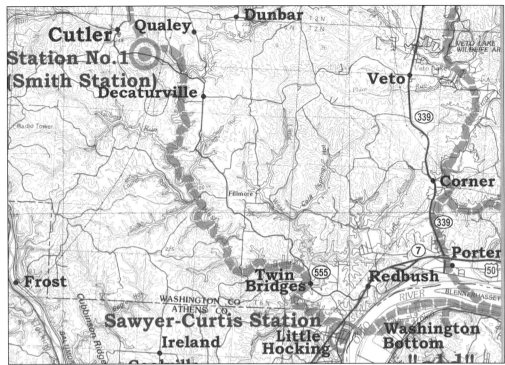

SAWYER-CURTIS TO SMITH STATION. Fugitive slaves passing through Little Hocking usually came from one of the places along Washington Bottom: the R. Edelen, J.H. Harwood, or George Neal Sr. Plantations. Occasionally they were from Blennerhassett Island Plantation or Parkersburg or one of the downriver places, and once in a great while, they were from somewhere deep in Virginia and at the end of a long journey already. But wherever they came from, they were normally guided north through Smith Station below Cutler when they left.

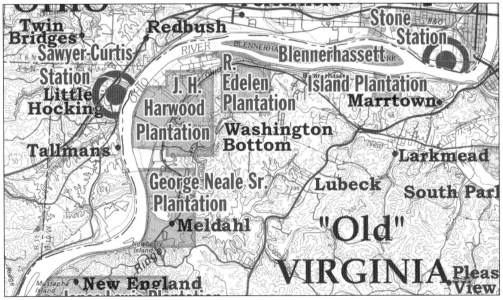

PLANTATIONS ON WASHINGTON BOTTOM.

SMITH (CUTLER) STATION. The homestead that was once known as Underground Railroad Station No.1, Smith, or Cutler Station is located one mile south of Cutler on SR 555 in the hilly terrain of western Washington County. The farm house and former stationhouse was almost demolished recently to make way for a modern developer's dream. But at the 11th hour, some students of history bought the place and its historic marker and made plans to preserve it for us all.

In any event, being located one mile south of Cutler puts the place about 12 miles, or one night's walk, north of the Ohio River. James and Margaret Smith settled on the property in 1834. It was likely chosen for its location along a dirt road that was then an escape route and eventually became SR 555. They built a log cabin there and started Underground Railroad operations the same year. They then continued that work for 25 years. One of their sons, Joseph Smith, built the house pictured here in 1847, and the work continued as before.

THE MONUMENT TO STATION NO.1. This monument was erected by one of James Smith's grandchildren. In part, it was dedicated to the fine work done for the Underground Railroad by the grandparents. Fugitive slaves arriving at the Smith place were fed and hidden so they could rest and then guided up the road through Cutler and on north to William Hale's Station No.2 or Uriah Bailey's Station at Bartlett. According to the plaque on the monument, between 1834 and 1860, the Smith family and others involved in the operation of Cutler Station assisted more than 150 fugitive slaves, mostly coming from Sawyer-Curtis Station at Little Hocking on the Ohio River. During warm weather, those fugitives were hidden in caves on the back end of the Smith property. When it was cold, they were hidden beside the chimney in the attic of the new house.

THE PLAQUE AND THE SHERIFF'S STORY. The lower part of the plaque above was dedicated to work done by the sons of James and Margaret Smith, and that fact figures prominently in the following. At some point in the 1840s, the sheriff of Wood County, Virginia, rode up to the front of the house in a buggy. He should have had at least one Ohio law officer with him to make his presence legal, but he had two or three deputies instead, and he told James Smith Sr., who was sitting alone on the porch, that he was under arrest and was going to be taken to Wood County to stand trial for violations of the Fugitive Slave Act of 1793. Smith was of course guilty of breaking that law, but he told the sheriff, "That may be well and good but before we depart I suggest you look up and see what's in my window."

By this time, all five of Smith's sons had appeared in the windows above—one to a window and each with a rifle. Under the circumstances, the sheriff decided it would be expedient for him and his deputies to leave immediately, and no arrest was made that day. The five sons were William, Alexander, John, Joseph, and James Jr., and as you can see from the plaque, all five would fight for the north in the Civil War. The marker was erected by Dr. Howard Smith, a descendant, in 1935. It commemorates in plain words the contributions made by James and Margaret Smith and their sons to "the cause."

HALE BENCH MEMORIAL, 1941.

WILLIAM HALE STATION (STATION NO.2) BENCH DEDICATION. Before Cutler was built by the M&C steam railroad, many fugitives went from the Smith farm to the Little Hocking Southland Branch Station No.2 at the Hale farm south of Bartlett. The weathered memorial benchtop from the Hale farm (pictured below, left) is on display at Belpre's Historical Society Museum. That farm is gone now. The land has new buildings.

The following is excerpted from the September 15,1941, *Marietta Times* account of the dedication displayed above: "Between 1840 and the Civil War William Hale, a Quaker and staunch abolitionist was one of the leaders in the 'Underground Railroad' . . . His home was one of the refuge 'stations' in which slaves were hidden between rides on the 'railroad.' Mrs. Harriet Ross Walker, a granddaughter . . . said that about 350 slaves were helped to the next station by her Grandfather and Grandmother Hale, her mother Martha Hale Ross, and the rest of the family. 'They had to be very subtle and sly,' she said, 'as no one knew when a slave or slaves would appear and neither did they know when their masters would appear, perhaps ready with warrants for the arrest of the men who had the slaves in their homes or hidden on their property." Seven men from the Hale family fought for the Union in the Civil War.

BENCH ON DISPLAY. Almost obscured by a larger cousin, the Hale Memorial Benchtop now resides in the permanent display of Underground Railroad Lore at the Belpre Historical Society Museum.

CUTLER, OHIO. The Smith place was the station, but surviving accounts speak of the role played in operating the station by the "sizeable population of free blacks" that came to live in Cutler as it was created by work crews constructing that stretch of the Marietta and Cincinnati Railroad and then preparing for its grand opening in 1857. Of course once the M&C was open, Cutler was an Underground Station too. The picture above of downtown Cutler was taken around 1895. The U.S. Postal carrier on the left, Essau Harris, is the son of Underground Railroad Conductor Thornton Harris. The postman on the right is James Parsons. It is time again to return to the Ohio River and pick up another thread.

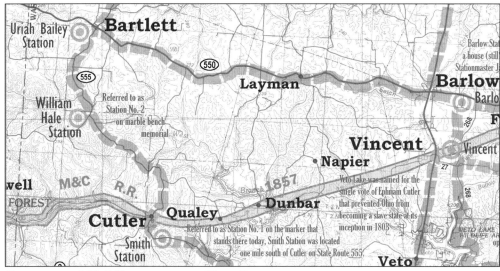

CUTLER, THE M&C RAILROAD, AND HALE STATION.

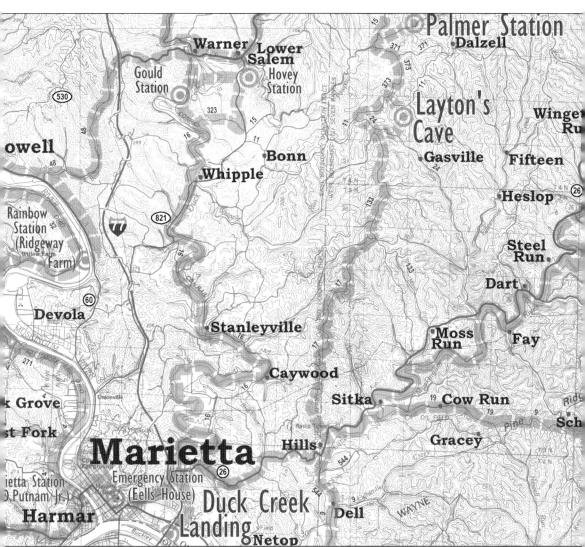

From the Ohio's Duck Creek Landing to Palmer Station. Palmer Station was part of an overland route from the middle years. The farmhouse is gone, but a record of what was done there survives. In addition to the references in stationmaster Jewett Palmer's obituary, Underground Railroad activities at Palmer Station were documented in letters from Palmer's son Jewett Jr. to his daughters. At least one of those letters, written in 1895, survived to become part of the Historical Archives Collection at WVU, at Morgantown. In that letter, Palmer Jr. describes taking breakfast to a runaway slave who was hiding in a thicket behind his father's house. Both participants were little boys at the time, and after fighting in the Civil War and the passage of more than 40 years, the important part for the author seems to have been that as a little boy, over the course of a half hour or so, he was able to see and accept the humanity of a little boy he encountered, the first black person he had ever seen, when he couldn't even understand his words.

THE REGISTER.

Thursday Morning, - - Oct. 2, 1873.

JEWETT PALMER, SR.

o

Another Veteran of 1812 Gone.

The subject of this sketch, whose death was announced in the REGISTER of September 18th, was born in the county of Grafton, in the State of New Hampshire, on the 18th day of May, A. D. 1797, and was consequently in the 77th year of his age, at the time of his death...

Though he never held official position outside of his township, he wielded an extended influence in the community. He was a man of general intelligence, a constant reader of the best newspapers, as well as of all valuable books that fell in his way, industrious and upright, of unerring judgment, a fearless adherent of principle, and a firm friend of the needy and of the slave. A well-known station on the Underground Railroad was kept by him, and many an anxious fugitive has blessed him as he stepped aboard the train for the next station.

In politics his quiet influence was perhaps greatest. Many young men of the neighborhood, whose fathers were bitterly opposed to him politically, side by side with "Uncle Jewett" at the polls, cast their first ballot for his candidates, at a time, too, when it required not a little courage to do so, for his were the Abolition candidates, whenever that party had a ticket in the field.

Voting for John P. Hale, in 1852, a young and enthusiastic admirer of Scott, and his military exploits, (who was unable to realize that the Whig party was even then dying from an "attempt to swallow the Fugitive Slave Bill,") asked him, why, as an old soldier, he did not vote for Scott. To which he replied, "You may not now understand my vote, but, should you live an ordinary life-time, you will witness the triumph of the *principle* for which I contend," little thinking that his own eyes should behold the triumph which he prophesied, in the removal of his country's curse.

PALMER'S OBITUARY. The document to the left is a portion of an obituary, Jewett Palmer's, printed in the *Marietta Register* in October of 1873. It says among other things that Palmer was constant in his politics all his life and died at age 77.

PATH TO LAYTON'S CAVE. Hidden in the woods today, much as it was 150 years ago, Layton's Cave is located over one ridge from and about a mile and a half south of Palmer Station. Palmer's farm and station in turn were located off of TR 361 about a mile south of the present village of Germantown. Layton's Cave was used by Jewett Palmer and his conductors as a backup shelter in which they hid fugitive slaves from bounty hunters and the law. The site today is privately owned and accessible by appointment only.

Map labels, reading across the image:

- 145 — Markey Station
- 834 — 289
- Flag
- Middleburg Station
- Middleburg
- 260
- Elk
- Road Fork
- Sycamore Valley
- Gem
- 303
- "Rockingham" John Curtis found
- The former family residence of Stationmaster and Reverend Joseph Markey. This abandoned house was once an active link in the chain of Underground Stations. But now it is a prime candidate for an archeological dig, with its debris filled cellar being exposed a bit more each year to the elements as its walls come tumbling down.
- In the fall of 1846 the Curtis brothers were fugitive slaves living in Colby's cave, unaware that they were surrounded by abolitionist homesteads.
- 564
- 260
- Blacksburg
- Aurelius Station
- MINES
- Harriettsville
- 565
- Lebanon
- Mar WAY
- Elba
- Kilmer
- NOBLE CO.
- 354
- Germantown
- 145
- 361
- Palmer Station
- Dalzell
- Warner
- Lower Salem
- 371

PALMER STATION TO MARKEY STATION. It was a journey of 11 or 12 miles if the fugitives went by way of Harrietsville, and as you can see from the map, this far from the Ohio they had entered an interlocking web of routes and stations. This book is headed to Markey Station because that is the option that was photographed the best. Actual fugitive slaves at Palmer Station could have gone on to Middleburg Station by way of Harrietsville or to Stafford or Woodsfield Stations by way of Lebanon and Marr. Topography was usually a determining factor as to where a route ran. Deciding which route to use was a more complex question. Where is the pursuit? How good are they? How high is the water running in streams along the way? How healthy are the fugitives? How rough a route can they take? Answers to all these questions were part of route selection.

STATIONHOUSE DOOR FROM THE SOUTHWEST. The house was small and set at the edge of a deep wood. Fugitive slaves were therefore boarded outside under the trees, except in very bad weather. It has totally collapsed now, but in these pictures taken in 1995, it is possible to see the one time home and Underground Railroad stationhouse of Stationmaster and Reverend Joseph Markey and family. The picture below was taken from the southeast. The station was also closely connected with Underground operations carried out through the many safehouses that made up Stafford Station.

MARKEY STATION.

HENRY BURKE INSIDE MARKEY STATION IN 1995. One evening, fugitive slaves hidden in a jumble of recently cut trees near the house were astonished to see their pursuers, led by their legal owner, make camp for the night within sight of those trees. The Reverend Markey and his family probably stayed inside where these pictures were taken that evening to avoid trouble. The slavers only stopped for the night before heading into Stafford in the morning (after one of their party missed discovering the hideouts by a couple of yards). The owner did hope to find his runaways there but was confronted instead by Stafford Stationmaster William Steel and a growing crowd of hostile armed abolitionists and left empty handed

STATIONHOUSE DOOR FROM INSIDE.

MARKEY STATION INTERIOR. The photograph on the right shows the fireplace from what was left of the parlor in 1995. At the time these photograph were taken, the cellar where fugitive slaves could be hidden in bad weather was half filled with soft debris.

ARCHEOLOGICAL TREASURE IN THE GROUND. The photograph on the left shows what was left of the fireplace from the kitchen in 1995. But as has already been mentioned, this building has now collapsed totally and been bulldozed flat. So we have an unexamined Underground Railroad station where events dramatic enough to receive mention in diary and newspaper accounts transpired. If ever there was a site that cried out for archeological attention, Markey Station is it.

INDEPENDENT STREET, STAFFORD, OHIO. "Freedmen" made up a large portion of the population. Most of the rest were active abolitionists. Stafford, Ohio, founded in 1834, was more a giant Underground Railroad station than a town with a station and anti-slavery sympathies. On a given day, any structure in the community might have been used to hide fugitive slaves, and in the 30 years before the Civil War, no fugitive slave who reached Stafford was ever recaptured. Stationmaster, mill owner, and town founder William Steel was famous as a "recognized leader" of abolitionists in Southeastern Ohio. He lectured and wrote extensively about the issue. He also ran for congress on the Liberty Party ticket and was among those all across the north who circulated a document known as the "Great Petition," in which all those signing promised to vote for Henry Clay, if only he would free the one slave he owned. At one point, Steel was informed that Virginia slave owners had put a price of $5,000 on his head. He remarked that he would be glad to take his head to them, if only the money would be placed in responsible hands.

STAFFORD'S CENTRAL HOTEL, *circa* **1895.** Pictured here from left to right are Phillip Marlbrough, a groom of horses; Warren Anderson; Roy Anderson; Henry Anderson; Grace Anderson, who ran the hotel; and Sarah Thompson (in the white dress), a helper.

MABLE AND ANNA CURTIS IN 1905 AT STAFFORD, FORMERLY STAFFORD STATION. People on the Underground Railroad arrived at Stafford from Hovey, Palmer, and Markey Stations having come up Duck Creek or the Little Muskingum River or even along the dirt road from Marietta. When they got there, a whole town was waiting. Anna and Mable Curtis (left) carried the sympathies of their grandfather "Rockingham" John Curtis and the rest of Stafford when these pictures were taken and for the rest of their lives. Stafford reached its peak population of 300 souls in the 1860s and 70s. By 1980, the population had dropped to 98. This diaspora took some families to Rainbow Creek in Washington County, to Zanesville in Muskingum County, to Barnesville in Belmont County, and eventually everywhere. Stafford was not alone. In the same period, Guinea and Lettown near Cumberland disappeared altogether.

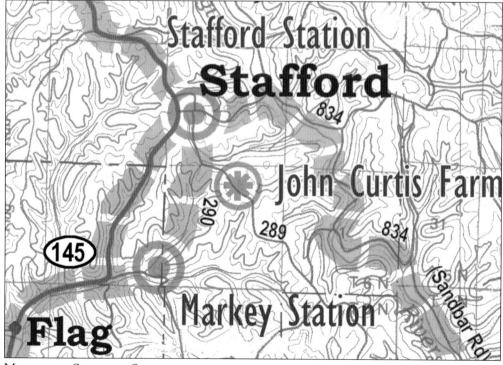

MARKEY TO STAFFORD STATION.

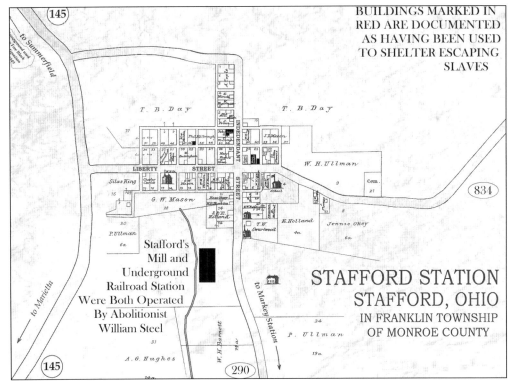

STAFFORD, A CITY OF SAFEHOUSES. Fugitive slaves leaving Stafford almost always headed up what later became SR 145 to Summerfield where the path fanned out again. Their conductors were Benjamin Hughs, Liberty Curtis, Timothy Cleveland, John Curtis, William Steel, and many others.

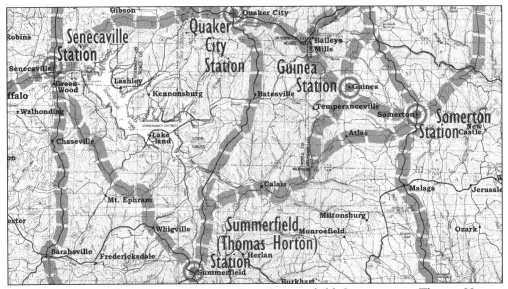

STAFFORD TO SUMMERFIELD AND BEYOND. From Summerfield, Stationmaster Thomas Horton sent people northwest to Senecaville, north to Quaker City, or northeast to Guinea or Somerton, and on to Collins Station at Barnsville. Guinea was a freedman's town.

The First Annual Stafford Reunion, circa August 1945

STAFFORD STATION REUNION. The annual Stafford Reunion is held at a park known as the Campground. Most of the migration to Stafford occurred after 1849 when Ohio repealed the law requiring a $500 security bond for "free" African-Americans entering the state. For many of the latecomers, it was only a place of transition, but it made an impression. In 1945, "free" African- American families at the reunion included Burke, Armstrong, Curtis, Freeman, Marlborough, Singer, Solomon, Woods, and Wooten.

ABANDONED HOMES. The movement of African-American families from places like Stafford, Guinea, and Lett Settlement was only partially coordinated with the national African-American migrations of the world wars. Many of these folks had not had a real choice in where to live since being stolen from Africa. Some of them left fine houses behind to move again (right). Could be they would have moved from Eden just to know they could.

ROSS CURTIS HOUSE. Located about 400 yards west across SR 145 from Markey Station, about two miles southwest of Stafford, Ross Curtis house is abandoned now. In its day, it had marble fronted fireplaces (shown at the bottom of the page preceding) and flock wallpaper in the back parlor (left). As we now know, the years ahead would bring economic and social pressures that would help move most of the descendants of Stafford's freedmen to Ohio's cities. It is well to know that some good and prosperous lives were lived here before that movement began.

FLOCK WALLPAPER.

COLLINS STATION (BARNESVILLE). Now the residence of the Welsh family, this home was once the main house of a farm owned by Underground Railroad Stationmaster Robert Collins. He was also a federal judge and joined with Quakers from Mount Pleasant and Barnesville in purchasing slaves from the slave auctions at Wheeling, Virginia, and setting them free. Collins Station was also the last documented stop on the Underground for the fugitive slave Jane, who escaped with her children from the Harness Plantation along Bull Creek.

STAFFORD TO GUINEA TO BARNSVILLE. Many of the fugitive slaves that reached Collins Station came through Guinea, which was six miles south of Barnesville.

QUAKER MEETING HOUSE AT MOUNT PLEASANT. Erected in 1814, this was the first Yearly Quaker Meeting House west of the Alleghenies. For nearly a century this meeting house played a crucial role in the propagation of the Quaker Faith in Eastern Ohio. From the first day of construction, it was a center of resistance to slavery. Funds were raised here when the Quaker community decided to buy slaves directly off the block at Wheeling's slave auction and set them free. "Book peddlers" were outfitted here for their recruiting forays deep into Northwestern Virginia, and actions were coordinated here among the many Mount Pleasant households that served as Underground Railroad safehouses during the years that slavery existed. After the Civil war, it was here that local Quakers gathered before heading south to build freedmen's schools. The connection between this station and the others in this book is the assistance it gave the others with their disruption of the Wheeling slave trade.

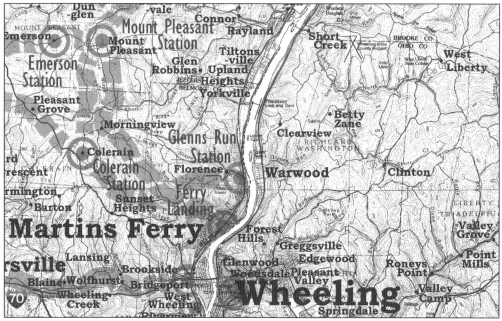

WHEELING TO MOUNT PLEASANT.

Three
"ROCKINGHAM" JOHN CURTIS

HIS LIFE AND TIMES.
"Rockingham" John Curtis, Henry Burke's great, great grandfather was born a slave in Eastern Virginia in 1830 but died a free man in southeastern Ohio in 1914. After escaping to freedom, Mr. Curtis worked as a mill hand, farmed, and (with the help of a loan from Ohio abolitionists) bought himself from his former owners, so as to be "legally" free.

He helped others to escape slavery by working as a conductor on the Underground Railroad, fought in the Civil War, and came home again to Stafford, Ohio. He then married, lived a long life, and died a patriarch, surrounded by his children and grandchildren on his own land. How did this happen? How could it be possible for this to happen? It is time to hear some stories and look into that old man's eyes.

THE ESCAPE OF "ROCKINGHAM" JOHN CURTIS. Sometime in 1846, John Curtis, age 16, and his younger brothers, Harrison, age 14, and Benjamin, age 13, escaped from a plantation in Rockingham County, Virginia. Actually, the younger boys were taken along by their brother John, who thought he had killed their master with a singletree and had to leave. The boys ran west and somewhere fell in with a lying rogue of a slave dealer who promised to help them find freedom while actually planning to resell them south. They crossed Western Virginia on the old Arlington Pike (today's US 50), which struck the Ohio River at today's Parkersburg, but they never reached that town themselves. Instead, the slave dealer's real work and his intended treachery was revealed to the boys at an inn near Ellenboro. Their innkeeper Luke Jago warned them that they were on their way to be resold. He also gave them good directions to a river crossing at St. Marys, created a diversion that allowed them to slip away unnoticed, and lied so effectively when their second escape was noted that the slave dealer was forced to split his party in two to search for them, sending half to Parker's Landing. It was a very impressive performance, but Mr. Jago, in addition to being an innkeeper, was secretly an abolitionist and a stationmaster on the Underground Railroad as well. So he may have practiced such things.

Meanwhile when John Curtis and his brothers reached the Ohio River, "The dogs were gnashing at their heels." They crossed the river, escaping the dogs and gaining a lead, but bounty hunters persisted and chased them all the way across Washington County into what is now Noble County. When they finally shed off their pursuers, at least temporarily, it began to snow. It also grew very cold. The Curtis brothers went looking for shelter away from the road at a place called Road Fork on what is now called SR 145.

They found Colby's Cave, a shallow pocket in the hillside to the west of the road. A bear occupied the cave already, but it is told that John Curtis killed the bear with a large piece of sandstone. The brothers ate the bear bit by bit, and used its hide to help keep warm.

They hid in that cave for more than two months to avoid the bounty hunters they thought were still searching for them. But eventually, they were forced to come to grips with other problems. One very cold night in November, the youngest Curtis brother, Benjamin, died of exposure. The next morning the ground was frozen, and Harrison and John didn't have any tools, so they carried his body out of the cave to a spot nearby and covered it with stones they pulled from the east fork of Duck Creek, which ran through the bottom below the cave site. Then they headed off downstream to search for firewood and food.

Benjamin's improvised burial cairn turned out to be his brother's salvation for shortly after they left, it was discovered by a party of abolitionists from Stafford. That party interrupted whatever they had been doing and followed the tracks left by John and Benjamin with an eye toward offering assistance to the survivors. John and Harrison, remember, were grieving the loss of their brother and still worried about pursuit. A glance at the map above shows they had made

JOHN CURTIS' ROUTE TO FREEDOM.

camp in the center of a web of sympathizers. But they had no way of knowing that, and no reason to put their trust in strangers. It must have been a real shock, therefore, to find themselves surrounded less than a mile downstream from the grave site and then helped by a group of men they had never met before in their lives.

These were the Stafford abolitionists, some of them from the Feltner family, and the help they gave to John and Benjamin Curtis was not limited to a meal and warm bed for the night. After several nights, during which they recovered from severe exposure and near starvation, the surviving brothers were offered jobs at the local mill. The man offering those jobs was the mill owner and operator, William Steel, the same William Steel described earlier in the section on Stafford. Steel and the Feltners arranged contact with the legal owners of the Curtis brothers back in Rockingham County. It turned out that John Curtis had not killed his master after all but only knocked him unconscious. After determining a price, Steel loaned John and Benjamin Curtis the funds needed to buy their own legal freedom papers. That loan was repaid with the Curtis brothers' wages. While Harrison Curtis never returned from the Civil War, John "Rockingham" Curtis did, and as has been mentioned, raised a family there, and called Stafford, Ohio, home for the rest of his days.

"Rockingham" John and Jane Early Curtis Family. This picture was taken on the family farm near Stafford in Monroe County, Ohio, *circa* 1898. Left to right are Anna Curtis Dau, Elizabeth Early Curtis (wife of Tom Curtis), Gladys Robinson Curtis (wife of Ed Curtis), "Rockingham" John Curtis (holding small horse in center.), Ed Curtis (holding beagles), and neighbor Henry Singer (holding big horse).

In the case of John Curtis, "the rest of his days" included many years in the era of photography. The photographs grouped on the following six pages, together with the pictures of Stafford, show the lives lead by "Rockingham" John Curtis and his descendants better than words could.

Laura Curtis. One of the daughters of John and Jane Early Curtis, Laura Curtis, was born in 1877 but died very young, at age 17, in 1894.

JANE EARLY 1848–1890. Jane Early Curtis was the wife of "Rockingham" John Curtis. (Photographed some time before 1890 by P.D. Cadawallader.)

ED CURTIS. Born in 1886, Ed Curtis was one of the sons of "Rockingham" John Curtis and Jane Early Curtis. Ed Curtis worked his parent's land until 1952 when he died in a fall from a wagon very similar to the one he is pictured driving here, on the same stretch of road. The road, unchanged until this day, is part of the Underground Railroad Route from Markey Station to Stafford.

HAM CURTIS. Ham in downtown Stafford, Ohio.

CLEM CURTIS AND HIS HORSE GINGER. Born in 1871, Clem Curtis was another of the sons of "Rockingham" John and Jane Early Curtis. Clem Curtis lived until 1947 and is pictured here in 1945.

JOHN HENRY CURTIS AND BELLE ALEXANDER CURTIS. John Henry Curtis was another of the sons of "Rockingham" John and Jane Early Curtis. In 1914, he had this picture taken of his wife and himself in Wheeling.

AUTHOR HENRY ROBERT BURKE. One of many great, great grandsons of "Rockingham" John Curtis, author Henry Robert Burke belongs in this album.

JOHN HENRY CURTIS AGAIN. Pictured above at the wheel of his 1912 Enger, John Henry Curtis had become a successful man when this picture was taken. Also pictured is Charles Early of Cumberland, Ohio, a first cousin of the driver.

CLEM CURTIS AGAIN. Appearing somewhat smaller when dressed for town, Clem Curtis is pictured here in 1945, standing in front of two buildings in Stafford. The one on the left was William Steel's, the one on the right was Curtis' house, and both served as safe houses for fugitive slaves when all of Stafford was a station on the Underground Railroad.

NIMROD BURKE'S OHIO TIES. Nimrod Burke was an Underground Railroad conductor and a Mariettan before the Civil War. He was descended of the Burke family that was part of 500 slaves freed in Virginia in 1791 by Robert Carter III. He went to war in 1861 with Major Melvin Clarke listed as a drover/scout on the rolls of the 36th Ohio. Clarke, who also built the "Castle" at 418 Fourth Street in Marietta (pictured above), gave Burke his first job in Marietta and taught him to read before the war. Clarke had a brief but successful soldier's career, being promoted to full colonel the day he died at Antietum in 1862. Burke stayed a scout with the always active Ohio 36th until it became possible for blacks to enlist as soldiers themselves in 1864. His enlistment paper for the 23rd Colored Infantry Regiment from March of that year is pictured on the right. Burke was made first sergeant of Company F of the 23rd almost at once. As a first sergeant, he served at the siege of Petersburg and with General Birney's Command in the army that pursued and encircled General Robert E. Lee and the Army of Northern Virginia at Appomatics Courthouse. He also witnessed the formal surrender. General Lee was beaten. He was also a relative of Robert Carter III and thought slavery to be a great wrong. He might have been pleased, therefore, to know that Nimrod Burke, the descendant of a man his ancestor had freed, was present on the other side.

VOLUNTEER ENLISTMENT.

District
STATE OF   TOWN OF

Columbia   Washington

I, _Nimrod Burke_ born in _Prince William_
in the State of _Virginia_ aged _Twenty Six_ years,
and by occupation a _Farmer_ Do HEREBY ACKNOWLEDGE to have
volunteered this _Twenty third_ day of _March_ 186_4_
to serve as a **Soldier** in the **Army of the United States of America,** for
the period of *THREE YEARS*, unless sooner discharged by proper authority:
Do also agree to accept such bounty, pay, rations, and clothing, as are, or may be,
established by law for volunteers. And I, _Nimrod Burke_ do
solemnly swear, that I will bear true faith and allegiance to the **United States
of America,** and that I will serve them honestly and faithfully against all
their enemies or opposers whomsoever; and that I will observe and obey the
orders of the President of the United States, and the orders of the officers
appointed over me, according to the Rules and Articles of War.

Sworn and subscribed to, _Washington DC._
this _23rd_ day of _March_ 186_4_   _Nimrod Burke_
BEFORE _Henry A. Scheetz_
         Capt & Pro Marshal DC.

I CERTIFY, ON HONOR, That I have carefully examined the above-named Volunteer, agreeably
to the General Regulations of the Army, and that, in my opinion, he is free from all bodily defects and
mental infirmity, which would in any way disqualify him from performing the duties of a soldier.

                                    J. W. F. Kearsey
                                    Surgeon of Board of Enrolment DC.
                                                    EXAMINING SURGEON.

I CERTIFY, ON HONOR, That I have minutely inspected the Volunteer, _Nimrod Burke_
previously to his enlistment, and that he was entirely sober when enlisted; that, to the best of my
judgment and belief, he is of lawful age; and that, in accepting him as duly qualified to perform the
duties of an able-bodied soldier, I have strictly observed the Regulations which govern the recruiting
service. This soldier has _brown_ eyes, _black_ hair, _copper_ complexion, is _5_
feet _9 1/2_ inches high.

                                    Henry A. Scheetz
                                    Capt & Pro Marshal DC.
                                                    RECRUITING OFFICER.

(A. G. O. No. 74 & 76.)

Mustered into the service of the United States, for three years or during the war, from date of enlistment, in Company 23', Regiment of US Col Troops Volunteers, on the 23 day of March 1864, at Washington —

Henry R. Scheetz Capt & Pro Marshal DC

NIMROD BURKE'S ENLISTMENT PAPERS.

NEGRO QUARTERS, ARMY OF THE JAMES.—[SKETCHED BY CAPTAIN L. L. LANGDON.]

NIMROD BURKE'S WAR SERVICE. First Sergeant Nimrod Burke was 25 years old and serving in the Army of the James when this lithograph was published in Harper's Weekly on February 25th, 1865. It is unlikely that the artist, Captain L.L. Langdon chose Burke's unit as the subject of his work, but Burke wintered in quarters like these in 1865 and participated in the horrific series of battles known collectively as the siege of Petersburg. John Curtis, then 35, was in the U.S. Army also, but serving in the Carolinas with the Third Colored Infantry. The two men would not become close until they both wed and had children, and Burke's daughter married Curtis' son, long after the war.

STAFFORD SCHOOL. Finally, the habit of cooperation built during those years insured that in 1915, Stafford, Ohio (first named Bethel by the abolitionists who founded it), would have the fully integrated school pictured on the left.

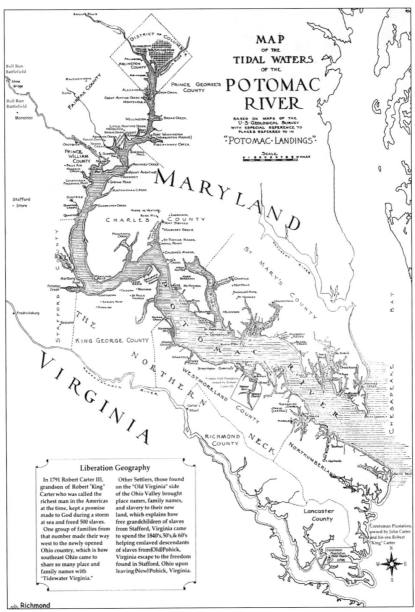

Liberation Geography

In 1791 Robert Carter III, grandson of Robert "King" Carter who was called the richest man in the Americas at the time, kept a promise made to God during a storm at sea and freed 500 slaves.

One group of families from that number made their way west to the newly opened Ohio country, which is how southeast Ohio came to share so many place and family names with "Tidewater Virginia."

Other Settlers, those found on the "Old Virginia" side of the Ohio Valley brought place names, family names, and slavery to their new land, which explains how free grandchildren of slaves from Stafford, Virginia came to spend the 1840's, 50's, & 60's helping enslaved descendants of slaves from (Old) Pohick, Virginia escape to the freedom found in Stafford, Ohio upon leaving (New) Pohick, Virginia.

LIBERATION GEOGRAPHY. In 1791, Robert Carter III, grandson of Robert "King" Carter, the "richest man in the Americas" at the time, kept a promise made to God during a storm at sea and freed 500 slaves. One group of freed families made their way west to the newly opened Ohio Country, which is how Southeast Ohio came to share so many place and family names with the "Tidewater" region of Virginia. Other settlers from the Tidewater, white settlers who brought slavery with them, were meanwhile moving into the Old Virginia side of the Ohio Valley. This is how free children and grandchildren of slaves from Stafford Virginia came to spend the 1840s, 50s, and 60s helping slaves from (Old) Pohick, Virginia, escape to the freedom found in a place they had renamed Stafford, Ohio. And it is how some of those slaves came to be escaping from a place called (New) Pohick, Virginia.

TUNNEL EXIT/WELL.

"TUNNEL" STATION. With apologies to anyone who expected to find information here on Tunnel Station immediately west of Marietta, the picture below is of a dig near Dayton. It is here because it relates to that odd notion that the Underground Railroad really ran underground. People have heard of tunnels from one place to the next, or from a house in some town to the local river, and they want to see it. The thing is, following French usage from their revolution, "underground" meant secret. Aside from short passageways between buildings, the tunnels people believe in couldn't have existed anyway. Oxygen, once it is consumed will not be replenished in a closed space. In places like Ohio there are toxic gasses underground that can seep in and turn any closed space into a death trap within days of its being dug. The equipment necessary for ventilating a tunnel from one end or the other without building air shafts along the way that would show was invented during the Civil War. Pictured below is a real Underground Railroad Tunnel being inspected by researchers. It is about nine feet long and went from a basement exit that was once hidden behind a false wall to an exit hidden in the side of a well shaft right outside the house. Fugitive slaves hid in the tunnel and used it to slip away from trouble.

WILLIAM PAYTON 1792–1919. It was said earlier that "Rockingham" John Curtis wasn't alone in building a long satisfying life. William Payton (on the right and below) lived 128 years. As a slave, he belonged to George Creel and his descendants at Davisville, Virginia. As a free man, he farmed in Decatur Township in Washington County, Ohio, and occasionally returned to Davisville for visits. Micajah "Cajoe" Phillips, also mentioned earlier, lived to 125. All three of these men had to "exercise and eat right" to survive their early years, but there is more to long, good lives than healthy habits. These men thrived in freedom after slavery was gone.

Head-Quarters Department of the Ohio,

CINCINNATI, MAY 26, 1861.

TO THE UNION MEN OF WESTERN VIRGINIA:

The General Government has long enough endured the machinations of a few factious Rebels in your midst. Armed traitors have in vain endeavored to deter you from expressing your loyalty at the polls. Having failed in this infamous attempt to deprive you of the exercise of your dearest rights, they now seek to inaugurate a reign of terror, and thus force you to yield to their schemes, and submit to the yoke of the traitorous conspiracy, dignified by the name of Southern Confederacy. They are destroying the property of citizens of your State, and ruining your magnificent railways. The General Government has heretofore carefully abstained from sending troops across the Ohio, or even from posting them along its banks, although frequently urged by many of your prominent citizens to do so. It determined to await the result of the late election, desirous that no one might be able to say that the slightest effort had been made from this side to influence the free expression of your opinion, although the many agencies brought to bear upon you by the rebels were well known. You have now shown, under the most adverse circumstances, that the great mass of the people of Western Virginia are true and loyal to that benificent Government under which we and our fathers have lived so long. As soon as the result of the election was known, the traitors commenced their work of destruction. The General Government can not close its ears to the demand you have made for assistance. I have ordered troops to cross the river. They come as your friends and brothers—as enemies only to the armed rebels who are preying upon you. Your homes, your families, and your property are safe under our protection. All your rights shall be religiously respected.

Notwithstanding all that has been said by the traitors to induce you to believe that our advent among you will be signalized by interference with your slaves, understand one thing clearly—not only will we abstain from all such interference, but we will, on the contrary, with an iron hand, crush any attempt at insurrection on their part.— Now, that we are in your midst, I call upon you to fly to arms and support the General Government. Sever the connection that binds you to traitors—proclaim to the world that the faith and loyalty so long boasted by the Old Dominion, are still preserved in Western Virginia, and that you remain true to the Stars and Stripes.

GEO. B. McCLELLAN,

Major General U. S. A., Commanding Department of the Ohio.

1861 OCCUPATION OF "WESTERN VIRGINIA." McClellan's occupation of the Little Kanawha Valley in 1861 was motivated by the need to keep the B&O rail line from Parkersburg to Grafton open in the face of guerilla opposition. The Union Army had enough force on the ground to do whatever it wanted in Parkersburg until the end of the war. But local slave owners took comfort from McClellan's posted statement (above), or they did until his troops enforced the peaceful opening of what they called the first black school in the South at Parkersburg, Virginia: Sumner School. Teaching African Americans to read and write was not a southern sympathizer's strategy.

Four

SLAVE OWNERS

BLENNERHASSETT ISLAND PLANTATION. The original, built with slave labor for Harmon and Margaret Blennerhassett, was a palace set like a jewel in its sculpted gardens. It burned in May of 1811. Slaves continued to work the large fields of the lower island until emancipation day. But the mansion was a ruin until 1985. Then, using dimensions from surviving sketches and the old foundation, a new mansion was built that hopefully looks like the one built in 1797. The palace was restored, and the new ferry follows the same course taken by the slave "Cajoe" Phillips when he rowed guests to the island in 1799.

Of course when slaves had that job, the first steamboats had not yet been built. The first owners used their slaves to raise vegetables and hemp and harvest mussel shells. Those operations have not been restored. They whipped slaves when they were displeased, but the whipping post is nowhere to be found. Still, history can be felt there.

The picture below was taken from the parking lot of a restaurant in Belpre that overlooks the island from the Ohio shore. The tail of the island extends for more than two miles down river from there, and that tail was often used as a river crossing aid by slaves escaping the area.

A SCHEME of a LOTTERY

For difposing of certain LANDS, SLAVES, and STOCKS,

belonging to the fubfcriber.

Priz.	→	Value.	CONTENTS of PRIZES.
1 of		£. 5000	To confift of a forge and geared grift-mill, both well fixed, and fituate on a plentiful and conftant ftream, with 1800 acres of good land, in King and Queen county, near Todd's Bridge; which coft 6000l.
1 of		1375	To confift of 550 acres of very good land, lying in King William county, on Pamunkey river, called Gooch's, part of 1686 acres, purchafed of William Claiborne, deceafed; the line to extend from faid river to the back line across towards Mattapony.
1 of		1925	To confift of 550 acres of very good land, adjoining and below the faid tract, lying on Pamunkey river, whereon is a good dwelling-houfe, 70 feet long and 20 feet wide, with three rooms below and three above; alfo all other good and convenient out-houfes; 1000 fine peach trees thereon, with many apple trees and other forts of fruit, a fine high and pleafant fituation, and the plantation in exceeding good order for cropping; the line to extend from faid river to the back line towards Mattapony.
1 of		1350	To confift of 586 acres, below the aforefaid two tracts; whereon is a fine peach orchard, and many fine apple trees; the plantation is in exceeding good order for cropping, and very fine for corn and tobacco, and abounds with a great quantity of white oak, which will afford, it's thought, a thoufand pounds worth of plank and ftaves.
65 of	£. 50	3250	To confift of 6500 acres of good land, in Caroline county; to be laid off in lots of 100 acres each.
4 of	75	300	To confift of 812 acres of good land, in Spotfylvania county, in the fork between Northanna and the North Fork, with a large quantity of low grounds, and meadow land; to be laid off in lots of 203 acres each.
1 of		280	A Negro man named Billy, about 22 years old, an exceeding trufty good forge-man, as well at the finery as under the hammer, and underftands putting up his fire: Alfo his wife named Lucy, a young wench, who works exceeding well both in the houfe and field.
1 of		200	A Negro man named Joe, about 27 years old, a very trufty good forgeman, as well at the finery as under the hammer, and underftands putting up his fire.
1 of		200	A Negro man named Mingo, about 24 years old, a very trufty good finer, and hammerman, and underftands putting up his fire.
1 of		180	A Negro man named Ralph, about 22 years old, an exceeding good finer.
1 of		220	A Negro man named Ifaac, about 20 years old, an exceeding good hammerman and finer.
1 of		250	A Negro man named Sam, about 26 years old, a fine chaferyman; alfo his wife Daphne, a very good hand at the hoe, or in the houfe.
1 of		200	A Negro man named Abraham, about 26 years old, an exceeding good forge carpenter, cooper, and clapboard carpenter.
1 of		150	A Negro man named Bob, about 27 years old, a very fine mafter collier.
1 of		90	A Negro man named Dublin, about 30 years old, a very good collier.
1 of		90	A Negro man named London, about 25 years old, a very good collier.
1 of		90	A Negro man named Cambridge, about 24 years old, a good collier.
1 of		90	A Negro man named Harry, a very good collier.
1 of		100	A Negro man named Toby, a very fine mafter collier.
1 of		120	A Negro man named Peter, about 18 years old, an exceeding trufty good waggoner.
1 of		190	A Negro man named Dick, about 24 years old, a very fine blackfmith; alfo his fmith's tools.
1 of		80	A Negro man named Sampfon, about 32 years old, the Skipper of the flat.
1 of		70	A Negro man named Dundee, about 38 years old, a good planter.
1 of		85	A Negro man named Caroline Joe, about 35 years old, a very fine planter.
1 of		110	A Negro woman named Rachel, about 32 years old and her children Daniel and Thompfon, both very fine.
1 of		70	A Negro woman named Hannah, about 16 years old.
1 of		75	A Negro man named Jack, a good planter.
1 of		75	A Negro man named Ben, about 25 years old, a good houfe fervant, and a good carter, &c.
1 of		120	A Negro man named Robin, a good fawyer, and Bella, his wife.
1 of		70	A Negro girl named Sukey, about 12 years old, and another named Betty, about 7 years old; children of Robin and Bella.
1 of		75	A Negro man named York, a good fawyer.
1 of		80	A Negro woman named Kate, and a young child, Judy.
1 of		60	A Negro girl, Aggy, and boy, Nat; children of Kate.
1 of		75	A Negro named Pompey, a young fellow.
1 of		110	A fine breeding woman named Pat, lame of one fide, with child, and her three children, Let, Milley, and Charlotte.
1 of		60	A fine boy, Phill, fon of Patty, about 14 years old.
1 of		50	A Negro man named Tom, an outlandifh fellow.
1 of		280	A Negro man named Cefar, about 30 years old, a very good blackfmith, and his wife named Nanny, with two children, Tab and Jane.
1 of		110	A Negro man named Edom, about 23 years old, a blackfmith who has ferved four years to the trade.
1 of		160	A Negro man named Mofes, about 23 years old, a very good planter, and his wife Phœbe, a fine young wench, with her child Nell.
1 of		50	A Negro woman, Dorah, wife of carpenter Jemmy.
1 of		35	A Negro named Venus, daughter of Tab.
1 of		25	A Negro named Judy, wife of Sambo.
1 of		20	A Negro named Lucy, outlandifh.
1 of		25	A Negro man named Toby, a good miller.
1 of		100	A team of exceeding fine horfes, confifting of four, and their gear; alfo a good waggon.
1 of		86	A team of four horfes, and their gear, with two coal waggons.
10 of	20	200	To confift of 100 head of cattle, to be laid off in 10 lots.

124 PRIZES £. 18,400
1716 BLANKS

1840 TICKETS at 10l. each, is £. 18,400.

Managers are John Randolph, John Baylor, George Washington, Fielding Lewis, Archibald Cary, Carter Braxton, Benjamin Harrison, Ralph Wormley, Richard Henry Lee, Thomas Walker, Thomas Tabb, Edmund Pendleton, Peter Lyons, Patrick Coutts, Neil Jamieson, Alexander Donald, David Jameson, and John Madison, Gentlemen.

The above LOTTERY will be drawn on Thurfday the 15th day of December next, at Williamsburg.

N. B. Not any of the cattle mentioned in this lottery, are to be under the age of two years, nor none to exceed 4 or five years old.

tf
BERNARD MOORE.

Managers are JOHN RANDOLPH, JOHN BAYLOR, GEORGE WASHINGTON, FIELDING LEWIS, ARCHIBALD CARTER BRAXTON, BENJAMIN HARRISON, RALPH WORMLEY, RICHARD HENRY LEE, THOMAS WALKE THOMAS TABB, EDMUND PENDLETON, PETER LYONS, PATRICK COUTTS, NEIL JAMIESON, ALEXANDER D LD, DAVID JAMESON, and JOHN MADISON, Gentlemen.

The above LOTTERY will be drawn on *Thursday* the 15th day of *December* next, at WILLIAMSBURG.

N. B. Not any of the cattle mentioned in this lottery, are to be under the age of two years, nor none to exceed five years old.

tf

BERNARD MOORE.

(*on opposite page*) **1768 FATHER GEORGE AND THE SLAVE LOTTERY.** Big lotteries were often used to raise capital in colonial times, as illustrated by this advertisement from the *Virginia Gazette* of Thursday, April 14th of 1768. In this lottery, for £10, a citizen could have a chance at winning a team of horses, a herd of cattle, several thousand acres of land, or any one or two or three of more than 50 human beings. These slaves were brought up in the early Virginian tradition of slavery, and so had been taught trades to increase their value, which they are listed by on the lottery prize sheet. In Virginia, before the debates about human rights that sprang from the Revolution, slave owners were often proud of being the owners of skilled, industrious human beings. They thought of themselves as being superior, rather than of their slaves as being inferior, and that attitude shows even in this lottery advertisement.

We no longer wager or sell human beings of course, and the finer differences among slave owners' attitudes have fallen by the wayside. But there is still a part of this advertisement that is startling for many folks today. The third man is listed as a "manager," or guarantor that the land, livestock, and slaves would be as valuable as advertised, was the "father of our country," George Washington (*enlargement of bottom portion of opposite image, above*).

At that stage in his life, his exploits as a surveyor not yet begun, the country he was to father not yet born, Washington was known only as a respected veteran of the French and Indian Wars. Of course, he was also a Virginia planter and (as he is described in this lottery advertisement) a "gentleman." So perhaps it was a gentleman's duty in 1768 to pledge his honor that a lottery was fair, and the prizes offered were as described.

STAFFORD County, *Auguſt* 20, 1768.

RAN away laſt *April*, from one of the ſubſcriber's quarters in *Loudoun*, (where he had been a ſhort time ſawing) a Mulatto ſlave belonging to *Samuel Selden*, jun. named *Peter Deadfoot*, though it is ſuppoſed he has changed his name, as he the day before attempted to paſs for a freeman, and had got as far as *Noland's* ferry, on his way to *Philadelphia*, by a forged paſs, in which he was called *William Swann*. He is a tall, ſlim, clean limbed, active, genteel, handſome fellow, with broad ſhoulders; about 22 years of age, a dark Mulatto, with a noſe rather flat than otherwiſe, very ſenſible, and ſmooth tongued; but is apt to ſpeak quick, ſwear, and with dreadful curſes upon himſelf, in defence of his innocence, if taxed with a fault, even when guilty; which may be eaſily diſcovered, by any perſon's taxing him with being run away. He is an indifferent ſhoemaker, a good butcher, ploughman, and carter; an excellent ſawyer, and waterman, underſtands breaking oxen well, and is one of the beſt ſcythemen, either with or without a cradle, in *America*; in ſhort, he is ſo ingenious a fellow, that he can turn his hand to any thing; he has a great ſhare of pride, though he is very obliging, is extremely fond of dreſs; and though his holiday clothes were taken from him, when he firſt attempted to get off, yet, as he has probably paſſed for a freeman, I make no doubt he has ſupplied himſelf with others, as ſuch a fellow would readily get employment; it has been reported that he was ſeen on board a veſſel in *York* river, near *York* town; but for my own part, I ſuſpect that he is either in *Prince William* county, *Charles* county in *Maryland* (in both which places he has relations) or in the neighbourhood of *Wincheſter*. Whoever apprehends the ſaid ſlave, and conveys him to me in *Stafford* county, ſhall receive, if taken within ten miles of my houſe, Five Pounds; if above fifty miles, Ten Pounds; and if above one hundred miles, Twenty Pounds reward, beſides what the law allows.
THOMSON MASON.

Cumberland, Sept. 29, 1768.

RUN away from the ſubſcriber, a Negro man named HARRY, who is about 5 feet 8 or 9 inches high, a very ſenſible artful fellow, that ſpeaks quick and plain, underſtands a little of the carpenter's buſineſs, is a good waterman, and has been much uſed to work on board of ſhips, at *Cumberland* town, in the time he belonged to Mr. *Richard Littlepage*. He has a wife in the neighbourhood of the ſaid town, where I have good reaſon to believe he has reſorted ever ſince he has been run away, and might be eaſily apprehended. If he leaves thoſe parts, I am apprehenſive he will endeavour to make his eſcape by water, therefore deſire all perſons, particularly maſters of veſſels, not to harbour or entertain the ſaid Negro.

Alſo about the ſame time, a young Negro man named TOM, about 6 feet high, has a roguiſh look, and has loſt part of one of his ears. He has been ſeen in *Nanſemond* and *Norfolk* counties, and is ſuppoſed to be about the *Diſmal Swamp*. Whoever conveys the ſaid runaways to me, ſhall have 5 l. reward for each.
JOHN MAYO.

ALSO 1768, EARLY RUNAWAY NOTICES. Sixty such runaway slave notices came from one newspaper in one ten month period before the Revolution. It is interesting to note that in these pre-revolutionary runaway notices, slave owners show no hesitation in praising the abilities, judgment, and industriousness of their "property" to the skies. They are proud to own such fine people. By 1805, after a national discussion of human rights, most of their sons would be describing their slaves as lazy, malevolent, slow-witted children to justify their continued ownership—and many of their sons would believe it.

SLAVE TRANSFER

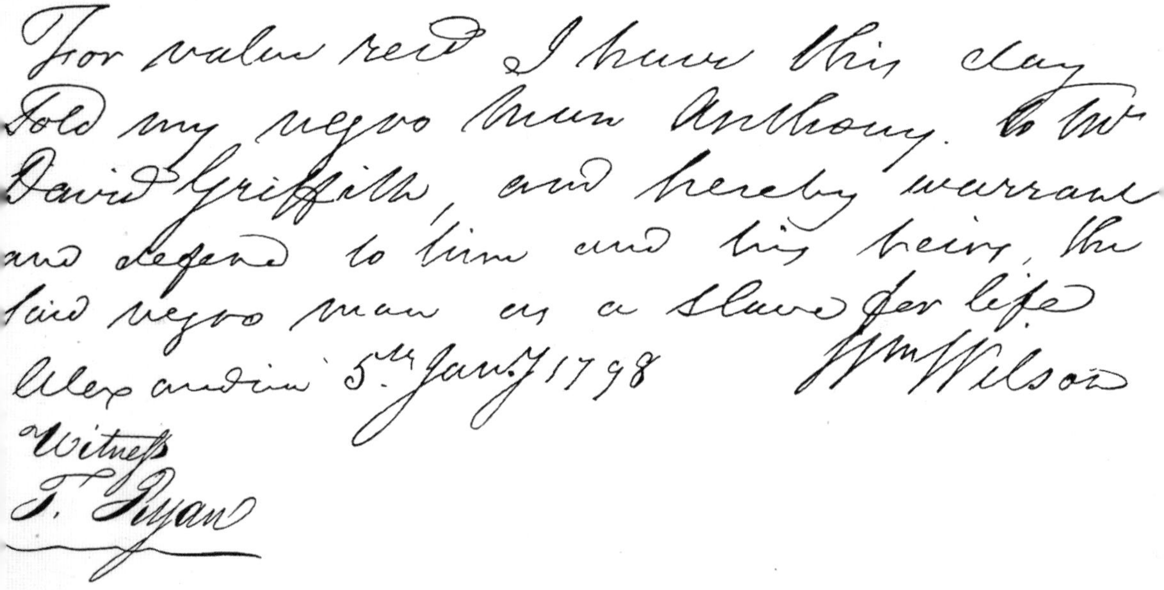
For value recd I have this day
Sold my negro man Anthony to Mr
David Griffith, and hereby warrant
and defend to him and his heirs, the
said negro man as a slave for life
Alexandria 5th Jany 1798 Wm Wilson
Witness
T. Ryan

"For value recd. I have this day sold my negro man Anthony to M. David Griffith, and hereby warrant and defere [sic] to him and his heirs, the said Negro man as a Slave for life."

–The transfer is dated July 5, 1798.

Not to be confused with freedom papers, the document above amounted to a title to a human being. Possession of such a document gave its holder the right to use any means including starvation, torture, and murder to control their property. (From the collection of Henry Burke.)

SLAVES PLANTATIONS IN ONE SEGMENT OF THE OHIO VALLEY. This map only covers a small part of the western edge of Old Virginia, and even so, it is woefully incomplete. Information about slave plantations remains fragmentary.

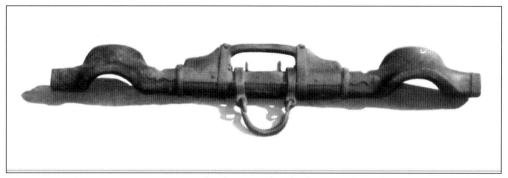

SLAVE YOKES AND SLAVE COFFLES. The first "civilized" slaves in the Ohio Valley were walked in from Pennsylvania in coffles in 1770. The leg irons of Hollywood movies look historic, but captives being moved across rough country have been tied together by the neck since Roman times. The yoke pictured here is from the collection of Warren E. Offenberger; it was made around 1800 and was bought at auction in West Virginia.

1799 WILLOW ISLAND PLANTATION. Willow Island is gone now. It was dredged away to make room for the Willow Island Dam. A map prepared under the direction of John Wood in 1824 shows it as having been very close to the Virginia shore of the Ohio and names it, along with Eureka and Broadback Islands, as one of the "Three Brothers Islands."

The house built by Alexander Henderson when he settled on the island with his family and slaves in 1799 is still there. Being a substantial structure with some historical significance, the house was moved so that it could be preserved. It stands today inside the government fence that surrounds the dam. It is pictured above. The Hendersons were a big acquisitive family with extensive holdings already in the Tidewater region of eastern Virginia. The same year they settled Willow Island, they began work on another tract downstream below the spot that later became Williamstown. That tract was eventually turned into another slave plantation.

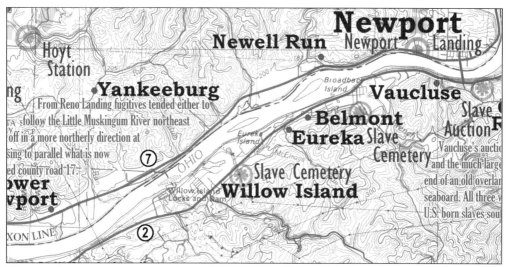

WILLOW ISLAND.

The following are the names of the Slaves Sent by Alexr Henderson Esqr of Dumfries, with Henry Summers, for the purpose of effecting a settlement on the Little Kanaway River. ——

Hary Bull . . . . 48 Years old or 49
Suckey his wife . . . 36 or 37
Hethy . . . . 9 }
Lucy . . . . 7 } their children
Sarah 6 mo
Abram (drowned in Kankawa 13th October 1799) 24 Years old or 25
Hannah . . . . 19 or 20
Davy her child 18 mo
John Dingo . . . . 11 }
Stephen . . . . 9 } Brothers

Jany 1st 1799 ——

Tom Hanna's Son born 20th March 1799
Daniel Suckeys Son born 27th July 1800
Jimemy Hannahs Daughter born in the Winter 1800-1801

"The following are the names of the slaves sent by Alex Henderson Esq. of Dumfries, with Henry Summers for the purpose of affecting a settlement on the Little Kan hauay [Kanawha] River.

"Harry Bull	48 years or 49
Suckey his wife	36 or 37

Their children:

Hethey	9
Lucy	7
Sarah	6 months
Abram	24 years or 25
(drowned in Kanhauay 13th October, 1799)	
Hannah	19 or 20
Davy her child	18 mo

Brothers:

John Dingo	11
Stephen	9

JANY 1ST 1799

"Sam Hannah's Son born 20th March 1799
Daniel Sucky's Son born 27th July 1800
Jememey Hannah's Daughter born in the winter 1800–1801"

The page reproduced on the left is from the plantation journal of Dumfries Plantation, which was located near the birthplace of Robert E. Lee in the Tidewater region of Virginia. That journal and the other documents that immediately follow are from the Henderson Hall Collection, which remains at Henderson Hall south of Williamstown, West Virginia. They are reproduced here with permission of the current resident/descendant owner, Michael Ralston.

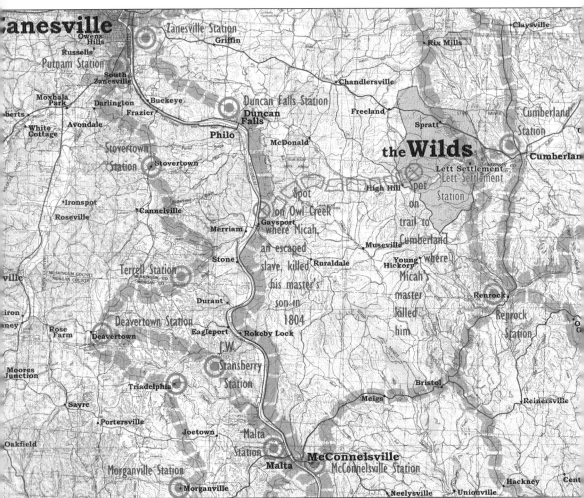

1804 SLAVE MURDER. In 1804, most of the Ohio and Muskingum River Valleys were still the untracked wilderness described earlier in this volume. The only dependable means of travel across this dark land was still by water. There were still hostile Native Americans, about, and each European-style settlement with its cleared ground still seemed more an island than part of an advancing frontier. For these reasons, two fugitive slaves apparently felt safe staying at the farm owned by William Craig on Owl Creek, which was about a half mile upstream from its mouth on the Muskingum River. No one really knows how they felt of course. It is one of the frustrations of studying actual history. In any event, before running away, these two slaves worked for a man named Williams at his settlement on the east bank of the Ohio River, directly across from the spot where the Muskingum River enters the Ohio from the west. They did run away one day, or rather paddled away, in one of the boats or canoes Williams kept, or had them keep, at his landing. It is fairly certain that they went directly across the Ohio and straight up the Muskingum because that route would have provided a fast exit without being the most likely course. But nobody saw them go, and so again, nobody knows for sure. Eventually, when they had paddled up the Muskingum River for a long day or so, they stopped and met a farmer who said they could stay there as free men, and they stayed.

They were only about 30 miles up river from the place they had escaped, Williams Station, Virginia. But they felt safe enough to stay there for some time and safe enough to show themselves in the presence of the occasional visitor. So maybe the two fugitives were unlucky.

Or maybe they had not understood that the population growth on the frontier meant an end to real isolation. Or maybe they were betrayed. It didn't really matter if any or all of the above was true because one of the people they felt safe enough to show themselves to was a canoe traveler heading down the Muskingum.

He either gossiped too much about matters he may not have fully understood or willfully reported the fugitives' location to their legal owner or one of his people. Again, it didn't really matter. One of the things that did matter was that their legal owner was Joseph Tomlinson II, of Grave Creek Plantation below Wheeling, Virginia, and he was visiting Williams Station when the canoe traveler arrived.

Tomlinson gathered together one son and three sons-in-law and the five men headed up the Muskingum to recover their "stolen property." When the slavers reached Owl Creek, William Craig shouted a warning. The two fugitives started to run, but Tomlinson's son Robert was faster than the slave named Mike and caught him and knocked him to the ground with a clubbed rifle. Mike got up and Robert knocked him down again. This went on for a time and may even have fit within the framework of "normal" slave and master relations. But eventually Mike, who was the same age as Robert, and had been raised side by side with him at Graves Creek, lost control and killed Robert with the knife he carried on his belt. The other slave escaped during the fight and disappeared unnamed from the Tomlinson's story, but Mike was captured. They tied Mike to a horse and started back overland to Williams Landing. They camped for the night along a stream, later called Negro Run, about three miles west of Cumberland on land that is now part of a game preserve known as the Wilds. Others were camped there. Somebody lit a fire and men gathered. There, in front of witnesses who later reported the incident to the authorities, the Tomlinsons executed and partially buried the slave Mike.

Some time later, after a coroner's inquest concluded that Mike might have been murdered, the governor of Ohio tried to have Joseph Tomlinson II extradited for a deposition. But Virginia's governor denied the request, and Mike's bones were left, said other witnesses, to scatter on the trail.

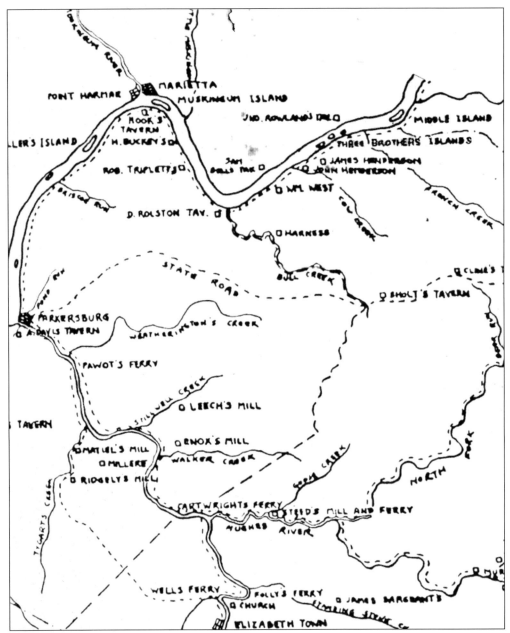

DETAIL OF JOHN WOOD'S MAP OF WOOD COUNTY PREPARED IN 1824. In addition to showing the Three Brother's Islands with the lower of the three still where it once was, this map puts Hook's Tavern in the spot where William's Landing was in 1804 and shows the first settlement on the Harness plantation as being roughly where the town of Cluster is today. It also locates two Henderson holdings without mentioning the one on the facing page, which hadn't been built yet when the map was made. It also reveals a general interest in taverns that would look out of place on a map prepared by a government official today.

1826 HENDERSON HALL (POHICK) PLANTATION. Pictured above and built with slave labor by George Washington Henderson and his wife (Elizabeth Ann Tomlinson,) Henderson Hall is an expansion of their second home, the structure they built in 1836, also with slave labor. The smaller, two-story back wing was completed 10 years after their arrival as newlyweds in 1826 on land just downstream from the Tomlinson property at William's Landing. Their first home was a wooden structure of some kind. They had named the plantation Pohick back in 1826, after an old Henderson family place in eastern Virginia's Tidewater region. It wasn't until they'd finished adding the larger three-story front section in 1859 that they took to calling the big house Henderson Hall.

IN FRONT OF THE BIG HOUSE. The land tends to spill down toward the river.

HENDERSON HALL. Both George Washington Henderson and his wife Elizabeth Ann (shown below) were second-generation "planters" in the Ohio Valley. George's father Alexander founded a plantation upstream at Willow Island on the Ohio River in 1799. He returned to his father's place, Dumfries, in Eastern Virginia to take a bride, Jane Lithgow, in 1801. He finally settled in at the Willow Island property the same year. Elizabeth Ann's father was Joseph Tomlinson III, one of the three surviving sons of Joseph II who executed the slave Mike by Negro Run near Cumberland in 1804.

Henderson Hall (pictured above in a view that allows one to see both the original homestead and the large frontal addition) remains as the best maintained and best documented plantation house in the region. It is open to the public for regularly scheduled tours.

THE HENDERSONS.

HENDERSON BOTTOM. The corn crop you can see in the foreground is growing in Henderson Bottom (under continual cultivation since 1836), a section of Pohick Plantation, and part of the slave holding Commonwealth of Virginia until the opening days of the American Civil War. The hills in the background are across the River in Ohio where it has been illegal for one human being to own another since the formation of the Northwest Territory in 1787. Fugitive slave laws passed by the federal government made Ohio less than free, but until the Civil War, the bottom was south of the Mason-Dixon Line, and the hills beyond were north of it.

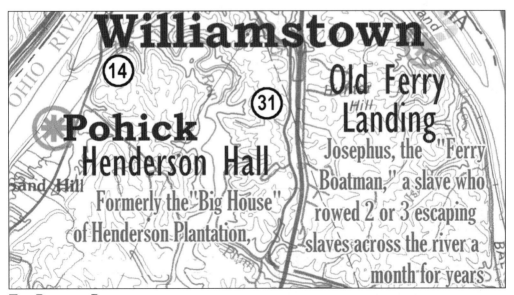

THE ROAD TO POHICK.

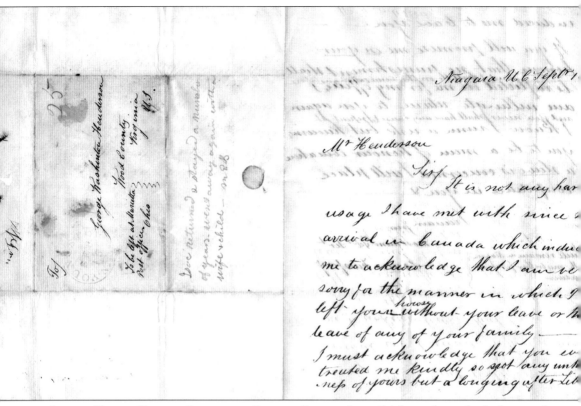

LETTER FROM A FORMER SLAVE TO A FORMER OWNER. Isaac Fairfax, a slave who had escaped from Henderson Hall Plantation in the 1840s and traveled to Canada by way of the Underground Railroad, penned this letter to his legal owner, George Washington Henderson, about a year later. The penciled note below the address reads: "Isaac returned and stayed a number of years went away again with a wife and child m. P H."

The letter itself reads:

"Niagra U.C. Sept. 13th

Mr. Henderson Sir/It is not any hard usage I have met with since my arrival in Canada which induces me to acknowledge that I am very sorry for the manner in which I left your house without your leave or the leave of any of your family. I must acknowledge that you ever treated me kindly so not any unkindness of yours but a longing after Liberty . . ."

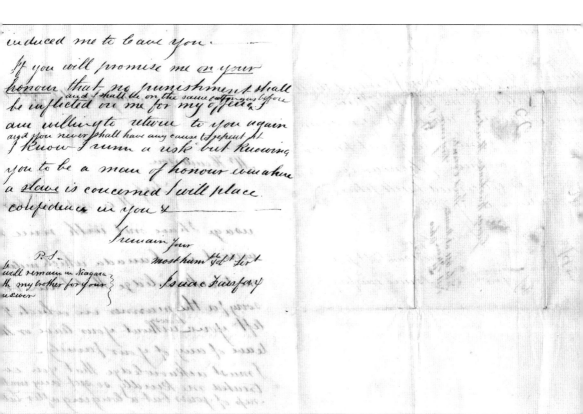

". . . induced me to leave you. If you will promise me <u>on</u> <u>your</u> <u>honour</u> [sic] that no punishment will be inflicted on me for my offense and I shall be on the same footing as before I am willing to return to you again and you never shall have any cause to repent it. I know I run a risk but knowing you to be a man of honor even where a <u>slave</u> is concerned I will place confidence in you X. I remain your most humble & ob. ser. Isaac Fairfax

"P.S. I will remain in Niagra with my brother for your answer."

The Henderson Hall Collection includes plantation work orders and ballots from the Lincoln election. It is held in a climate-controlled room in the restored mansion. It is a significant historic resource that, as of this writing, has never been cataloged.

> Jackson Oct 29/47
>
> Dear Sir
>
> I promised to write to you in regard to the slave Market which I now do There is a great demand with advanceing prices the rates ar as follow. Men No1 $800. To 2 $6.50 & None under $5 00, Women No 1 $7 00. No 2 600 down to 500. those Nos not to be above 40 & from 22 years the Women from 18 to 35 years of age Boys from 12 to 18 years of age are from 4 to 500 dollars that is more in the appearence of the Slave Girls from 12 to 18 very much in the manners & whare Raisd in or out doors Families are in demand whare parents is not past middle age in this country say 40 years old There is not been any brot to this Market this Season yet & if you have not disposd of yours yet you would do well to try this place in December or Janwary if you Was here Now you could sell fifty in 2 months This is not my own Judgment but the opinion of a Trader who has retird from the busines With a golden Treasure of about 100_ 000 &c &c

"Men No.1 $800 No.2 $650 & none under $500.
Women No.1 $700 No.2 $600 down to $500 . . .
Boys from 12 to 18 years of age are from 4 to 500 dollars . . .
Girls from 12 to 18 very much in the manners & whether
raised in or out doors. Families are in
demand whose parents is not past middle age . . ."

PRICE LIST. George Washington Henderson was the lawsuit-filing slave owner mentioned in the earlier section on David Putnam Jr. Included in a letter from Thomas C. Beason of Jackson, Mississippi, the price list reproduced on the left was used by Henderson in the lawsuit he filed later that year against Putnam in the Washington County, Ohio, Common Pleas Court. The suit alleged that Putnam had incited and abetted the escape of nine slaves and asked for either their return or adequate compensation. Putnam did help the slaves and clearly violated the Fugitive Slave Law, but the times (in Ohio) were changing, and he never had to pay Henderson a dime. The letter is dated "Oct. 27, 1847."

THE GLORY YEARS: HENDERSON HALL IN 1891. The slaves who built it may have been gone, but before the "new" road was built all travelers between Williamstown and Parkersburg still passed in front of the stately mansion house on the hill. (Photograph by Ernst Thoria.)

HENDERSON HALL TODAY.

KANAWHA SALINES. The Kanawha Salines referred to in the ad above was an area along the Kanawha River bottoms near Charleston, Virginia. It was a sort of early American industrial park featuring good access to transportation, good building sites for factories, and slaves available to lease. The hardware for the slave yoke seen earlier, which is estimated to date from around 1800, might well have been manufactured in Kanawha Salines by the fathers of those runaways in the ad.

LATER RUNAWAY NOTICES. The style changed greatly as the decades passed, but the runaway notice from the *Marietta Intelligencer* to the right and the one from the *Athens Messenger* below were typical for the 1820s and 30s. Note that by now, praise for the runaways has disappeared. These notices were a regular feature of American newspapers for 300 years. They are useful in tracking the changing shape of public attitudes towards slaves and in tracking the changing shape of the nation.

Five

WASHINGTON COUNTY STORIES

STONE'S OVERLOOK, SOUTH PARKERSBURG, VIRGINIA. That white house in the center of the frame across the river was an Underground Railroad Station from around 1810 to around 1861. It was Stone's Station at Belpre, Ohio. All those years ago, fugitive slaves and their conductors came to this spot to watch for a light in a certain window in that house. If the light was there, it meant the coast was clear, and they could slip down the hill and across the river without fear of capture. On the other side, they might be hidden at Stone's Station, or they might be passed up the line to Vincent or Barlow Stations. Either way, when it came time to move again, they would be guided further north by local conductors who knew the ground. The system was risky, but it worked and many people were freed.

FUGITIVES AMBUSHED AFTER MIDNIGHT ON THE OHIO SHORE AT BELPRE. The scene above is the Ohio shore at Belpre on the night of July 9th, or rather the morning of July 10th, 1845, at about 2:00 a.m. The men waiting on shore are Virginia slave owners lead by John H. Harwood and his son George. They are all heavily armed. The people in the canoes are one preacher and six slaves attempting to runaway from Harwood's Plantation on Washington Bottom. The slaves were Daniel Partridge, Frederick Gay, his wife, and their three children. Out of sight from the slave owners, over where the canoes are pointed, there are five members of the Underground Railroad. They are Daniel Garner, Creighton Lorains, Mordecai Thomas, Nathan Stanton, and Titus Shotwell. They are Ohioans, there to assist the fugitives in their flight. This has been arranged by the preacher, a traveling preacher named Romain, who functions as a contact agent for the Railroad. But this time someone has turned informant. When the canoes reach shore the five Ohioans grab the baggage, the two adult male fugitives grab the smaller children, and everyone heads up the steep bank. At this point the Virginians step out of the bushes and throw down. Daniel Partridge, the only slave who will escape, drops the child he is carrying and slides under the roots of a large fallen tree. He hears one of the Ohioans say, "Don't stab me—shoot me if you dare." He hears a "scuffle." He hears a shot fired from a pistol.

106

When the shot is fired, the scuffling stops. Nathan Stantan, Titus Shotwell, and the preacher slip away into the darkness like Partridge. But the other five slaves and three of the Ohioans are loaded into boats and rowed back to Virginia. One of the Ohioans is heard protesting against being taken across the river to be tried by their "bloody slave laws." The five recaptured slaves are returned to Harwood plantation where whipping and facial branding are the punishments for attempted escape. The three captured Ohioans, Daniel Garner, Creighton Lorains, and Mordecai Thomas are thrown in the Wood County Jail. Parkersburg, Virginia, the town where that jail is located, prepares to resist an expected attack by Ohio's Militia. That attack never comes, but the three Ohioans are held without bail for six months. Calling out the Ohio Militia is discussed. And nervous Virginia Militiamen shoot and kill the Parkersburg town bull while patrolling at night. The case of the three Ohioans is eventually tried before the Virginia Appeals Court in Richmond. Because it appears that the defendants had to be illegally abducted from Ohio before they could be charged with anything, no verdict is reached. Finally a special session of the court is held in Parkersburg at which bail is set, but the "Garner Case" (as Richmond's Court of Appeals has tagged it) is never called for trial. The three Ohioans pay their bail and go home, and tempers calm for a while.

STONE'S STATION CROSSING BY NIGHT. The illustration on the right reveals more than you could see on the river at night before electricity, which may be part of the reason that no fugitive crossing to Stone Station "with the light" was ever caught.

MODERN RIVER CROSSING. The photograph below was taken in 2003 at Marietta's landing. The tow is waiting for a crew replacement with its prow nosed into the island. But even without the tow, the light from the bridge changes everything .

overturned
butter
churn

wooden drainage
pipe section

assembly

painted
finished
product

COLONEL STONE'S FAUX CANNON
which fooled the Virginia Militia until the wind blew it over
in 1845

STONE'S FAUX CANNON. Shortly after the ambush in 1845, another incident occurred that brought Colonel Stone into the action. At the time, many Wood County residents believed that Ohio was looking for an excuse to storm across the river and destroy Virginia's way of life. So the condition of high alert instituted at Parkersburg the day after the ambush was more than a few sentry posts and trigger happy patrols. On the riverbank on the south side of town, a battery of cannon was installed and aimed north, directly across the river, at Colonel Stone's house. In the words of Henry Burke, "This infuriated Colonel Stone, who viewed this aggressive action through his binoculars. He commented to his colleagues, T.T. Hibbard, Danial Gross, and Pearley Howe, that he would retaliate. Since he did not have any real cannon, he put together a fake one and emplaced it in his front yard in the dead of the night. It was aimed south across the river at the battery threatening him when the sun came up."

The fake cannon (see the blueprint above) was convincing enough to fool travelers on the road who passed it on the morning of October 10th, 1845. And by all accounts it fooled the Virginia Militia across the river until it was blown over by a strong gust of wind a few days later.

General Rufus R. Dawes. A grandson of Ephraim Cutler who commanded Wisconsin's Bloody 6th Brigade during the Civil War, General Dawes once remarked that by 1855, traffic on the Underground Railroad through Marietta from across the river had been reduced to a trickle because most of the slaves over there who wanted to escape had already done so.

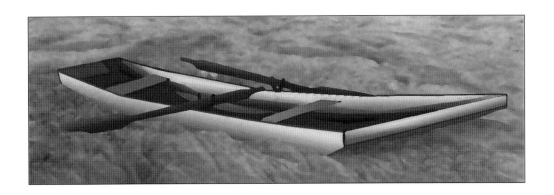

JOSEPHUS THE FERRY BOATMAN. For many years starting in the 1830s, the slave Josephus met one or two groups of fugitive slaves a month at sites on the south bank of the Ohio at night. He would then row them across the river and guide them to a meeting with their next conductor. It is known that Josephus was owned by the family residing at the "Box" plantation (and suspected that they were way too trusting), but no one now remembers which local plantation was known by that name. It is also known that his favorite landing site on the Ohio side was the mouth of Duck Creek. It therefore seems likely that he also used the rest of the old freight ferry crossing that ended there. This would mean that on some occasions, Josephus met his passengers above the wing dam that once stretched from Buckley's Island near its head to the Old Virginia shore. From there, he would row his charges across to the island in the dead water above the dam. He would then lead them across the island by way of the freight hauler's road. When the party reached the Ohio side of the island, Josephus would slide the boat back into the water and then coast down stream and cross current to the mouth of Duck Creek above Marietta.

Freight was moved by that route to avoid fighting the current with heavy loads of goods. Fugitive slaves moving by that route would have avoided the heavy loads of eyes on Marietta's then bustling riverfront where crew members of the many packetboats often kept odd hours. Josephus used other routes and landings. Fugitive slaves, after all, did not have much freedom of movement, and they could only be picked up at landings they could safely reach in a late night scramble.

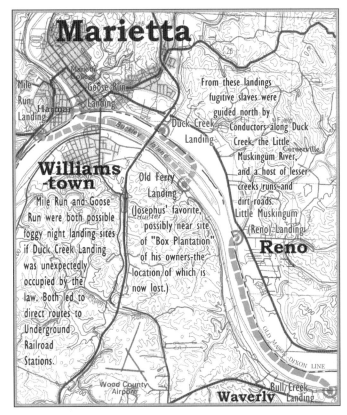

MARIETTA: RELEVANT HISTORY. By 1846, as seen here in an engraving by Henry Howe, Marietta was a hot bed of abolitionist activities. There were pro-slavery "copperhead" elements about. But there was also a ten-year-old chapter of the Anti-Slavery Society and a much older Underground Railroad network. The anti-slavers had the numbers, and there were reasons for that.

First, it was a Native American village (Mound Builder then Iroquois). Next, starting around 1700, it was a campsite for the French and the English. And finally, after the Revolution, it was a quietly abolitionist town, settled by New Englanders who liked all that history. It was sited on the edge of slave territory in a wilderness, and it was fortified.

Marietta was established on the east bank of the Muskingum River at its mouth on the Ohio in 1788, three years after Fort Harmar was built on the west bank by a detachment of "Continentals" led initially by Major John Doughty. The garrison at Fort Harmar included free blacks in its ranks from the beginning, as was evidenced by the birth of Marietta's first black child, James Davis, on March 6th of 1787. Marietta was made the first capitol of the newly established Northwest Territory a few months later, and (aside from assisting in a few land swindles) its citizens lived by the laws set down in the "Ordinance of 1787," which included a total ban on slavery. While Governor Arthur St. Clair made exceptions to that ban, it is also true that in Marietta and its surrounding area no slave was ever born or kept.

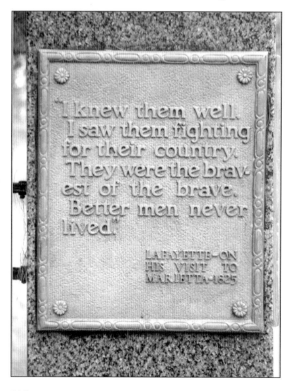

"I knew them well.
I saw them fighting
for their country.
They were the brav-
est of the brave.
Better men never
lived."

LAFAYETTE ON
HIS VISIT TO
MARIETTA 1825

LAFAYETTE RETURNS. When Lafayette visited Marietta in 1825, the sons of his old comrades had the Underground Railroad in full operation, but the Anti-Slavery Society was still more than 10 years away.

According to the *Marietta Gazette* members of Marietta's Anti-Slavery Society in 1840 included: John C. McCoy, John Crawford, E. Buttles, N. Ford, W.D. Emerson, A. Herlett, James Lawton Jr., George Putnam, C. Sharp, John M. Proctor, Eli Griffith, Simeon Duning, William Pitt Putnam, J.N. Ford, C. Tidd, J.D. Amlinm, John W.L. Brown, Julius Deming, Joel Tuttle, E. Gould, A.B. Nye, D.G. Stanleym, B.G. Stanley, W.P. Cutler, Thomas Ridgeway, and Joseph Hodgeman.

Those active in the Underground Railroad in the area included:

David Putnam Jr. (Marietta Station)	T.T. Hebbard (Belpre Station)	Reverend J. Markey (Markey Station)
Jewett Palmer (Palmer Station)	Danial Goss (Belpre Station)	James Smith (Cutler Station)
Jerry Jones (Marietta Station)	Perley Howe (Belpre Station)	Margaret Smith (Cutler Station)
Thomas Porter (Marietta Station)	Jonathan Stone (Belpre Station)	Aunt Jenny (Belpre Station)
Tom Jerry (Marietta Station)	Joseph Smith (Bartlett Station)	Uriah Bailey (Bartlett Station)
Dan Strather (Marietta Station)	Samual Hall (Constitution Station)	Joseph Smith (Bartlett Station)
Colonel John Stone (Belpre Station)	Judge Ephraim Cutler (Constitution Station)	Thornton Harris (Cutler Station)
The Huggins family (Marietta Station)	E.B. Hovey (Hovey Station)	R.M. Stimson (Marietta Station)

Most of these men and women were the children and grandchildren of the people who were protected by Fort Harmar.

Fort Harmar, *circa* 1789, Adapted from a Sketch by N.W.

GENIUS OF UNIVERSAL EMANCIPATION.

EDITED AND PUBLISHED BY BENJAMIN LUNDY, GREENEVILLE, TEN. AT $1 PER ANN. ADV.

"We hold these truths to be self evident, that all men are created equal, and endowed by their Creator with certain inalienable rights; that among these are life, liberty, and the pursuit of happiness." — *Declaration Independence U. S.*

No. 7. Vol. II.   *FIRST MONTH*, 1823.   Wh.le No. 19.

UNITED STATES' INFERNAL SLAVE TRADE.

"Ho! Columbia. Happy Land!"

SHALL THY FAIR BANNERS O'ER OPPRESSION WAVE?

(left margin) TO THE SOUTH-WESTWARD

(right margin) A GLORIOUS SPECTACLE!!!

TO THE AMERICAN PEOPLE.

The above is a faint picture of the *detestable traffic in human flesh*, carried on by citizens of this Republic in the open face of day, and in violation of the fundamental principles of our government, the maxims and precepts of Christianity, and the eternal rules of justice and equity. LOOK AT IT, *again and again* and then say whether you will permit so disgraceful, so inhuman, and so wicked a practice to continue in our country which has been emphatically termed THE HOME OF THE FREE.—"*Malum nascens facile opprimitur, inveteratum fit robustius.*"

¶A gang was lately paraded with the U. S. flag. (See *G. U. Eman.*—vol. 2. *p.* 59.)

PLAN FOR THE ABOLITION OF SLAVERY.

[It is considered expedient to re-publish the following, as many who patronise this work at present, have never had an opportunity of seeing it.]

For the purpose of effecting a gradual Abolition of Slavery in the United States, I would propose—

First, That the General government totally prohibit it in the districts over which Congress possesses the exclusive controul; to prevent its spreading over a greater extent of country, and consequently increasing in magnitude: and for the purpose of guarding more effectually against its extension, let a positive injunction be issued against the admission of any new state into the Union, hereafter, without an express provision against slavery in its Constitution.

Secondly—To prevent smuggling slaves into the country from abroad, to put a stop to the domestic or internal "slave, trade," and also to prevent the grievous crime of kidnapping free negroes, we let the transportation of them

BROADSIDE. Not a remarkable example of an abolitionist broadside except that the original of this one published in 1823 found its way to Washington County, Ohio, from its publishing point in Greeneville, Tennessee.

114

LADIES BOAT BAND. The specific names of the ladies pictured here are lost in time as is the actual name of their band. But it is known that they were all members of the Armstrong, Burke, and/or Curtis families and that as a group they played regularly for pay on the summer vacation stern wheel excursion boats that plied the Ohio and Muskingum Rivers in the 1880s.

FLOODING. Flooding was expected almost every year in the 1800s. Sometimes lots of people died. But having a local guide who knew the river and which was equipped to deal with it meant that Underground Railroad parties fared as well or better than other groups of travelers who had to handle the unknown without much assistance.

MARIETTA COLLEGE, SECRETARY HALL, AND THE ANTI-SLAVERY SOCIETY. In October of 1836, a crowd of armed pro-slavery toughs gathered for the purpose of making trouble for the first anniversary meeting of Marietta's Anti-Slavery Society. The meeting was to be held at the newly completed Baptist church at Fourth and Putnam Streets, across the intersection from the Gates of Marietta College. There had been trouble before. Several Society members had to leap out the windows of Harmar School and swim the Muskingum to reach home safely. This time the copperheads meant to shut the abolitionists down.

They had planned this action two nights earlier at a meeting at the county courthouse, deciding to first send a delegation asking the Society not to hold its meeting and second, if necessary, to end the meeting by force, or with the threat of force as had been accomplished at Harmar. They were also going to fall upon Society members and beat them as they exited the church. It was expected that the members would run for the "safety" of Marietta College, but the College could provide no real protection. In fact, the copperhead planned to follow their opponents onto the campus and use the resulting ruckus as a cover for burning the place down. Burning Marietta College down would be proper retribution, it was argued, because the school had provided aid and comfort to opponents of slavery and possibly even to fugitive slaves. Further, it had allowed an instructor, Samual Hall, to become secretary of the Anti-Slavery Society. It was hoped, also, that this fearsome act would scare local abolitionists into quitting their cause.

Unfortunately for the pro-slavery crowd, their courthouse meeting was informed on, the details of their plan became known, and they ran into an organized response. First, when the pro-slavery delegation arrived at the church, they were intentionally humiliated. Secretary Hall agreed to see them but refused to read their message. He also refused to touch it and this second insult lead to bitter denunciations and the loud declaration that, "abolitionists" were "beneath contempt." At this point, the delegation headed for the doors.

EVERYTHING HAS BEEN REBUILT, AND MOVED A BLOCK AND A HALF UP FOURTH STREET. This is the place the line was drawn in 1836—between the Baptist church and the college gates. They moved quickly. They still expected their plan to work. At the Harmar School meeting, after all, a bit of shouting combined with the mere threat of torching the wooden schoolhouse had worked quite well. But this time, waiting outside, in a group assembled after they had gone in, was a line of armed men. The line stretched from one side of the intersection of 4th and Putnam Streets to the other, separating the campus from the church. The men forming this line were a much larger group than the mob the copperheads had assembled (and much larger than Marietta's Anti-Slavery Society would ever get to be.) This second mob, mostly carrying stout canes, was lead by the town marshal and the mayor and fleshed out by local citizens, civic leaders, and most of the able-bodied males (faculty and student) of Marietta College.

One assumes that angry shouts died in the throats of pro-slavery demonstrators, but the record is silent on that point. What is known is that upon seeing their opposition, the Copperheads slipped away rapidly into the night. Then the mayor ordered a defensive perimeter around the entire college. Citizens and students stood guard all night long, and the college was not burned.

The next day when asked why he had suddenly taken a side on the hottest issue of the day, something he had avoided for years, the mayor said that no side had been taken, that he and a group of citizens had acted only to prevent mob violence. So the mayor was able, barely, to maintain a useful political fiction for a few more years. The other work being done at Marietta College went undetected or at least undisturbed.

That other work, as has been mentioned, was operating an emergency station at Eells House and providing conductors for Marietta Station. A private home that boarded students to the public eye, Eells House stood where the college Media Center stands now. It could be approached by fugitives hidden in a wagon or sneaking along Goose Run, and it could be left the same way.

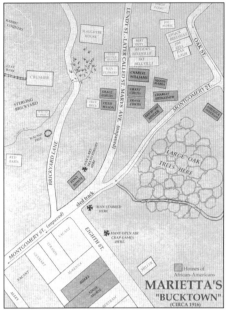

MARIETTA'S "BUCKTOWN" (CIRCA 1916)

MARIETTA'S BUCKTOWN, 1916. The original of this map was given to Henry Burke by a reader of his column. It shows "Bucktown" just before WWI when the neighborhood had probably already shrunk a bit. Bucktown grew during the Civil War and Reconstruction and shrank during the waves of black migration to major cities that accompanied both world wars. It is gone now, and Marietta's record in the area of civil rights is generally good. Like most other American towns, Marietta was segregated once, with separate churches and social clubs for "persons of color," and the record should show that, too. The area shown on the map centers on the intersection of Eighth and Montgomery. These days, schoolchildren travel those streets on their way to the city pool. The original map was drawn on a hamburger wrapper. It was redrawn by computer in hope of enhancing the original intent.

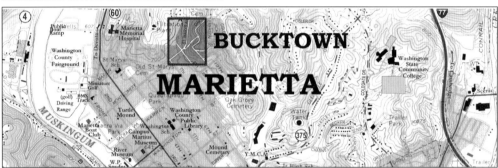

MARIETTA STATION REVISITED. This alternative view of Marietta Stationmaster David Putnam Jr.'s stationhouse was taken the day the last owner's things were auctioned off before it was torn down in 1953.

Six

THE ESCAPE
OF JANE

Collins
Station

Although there are some indications
that Jane and her family succeeded in
reaching Canada, her trip north is
documented only as far
as Collins Station.

After Stafford, aside from
encounters with rabid dogs
and wild animals Jane and her
children had no troubles
that have been recorded.

Guinea
Station

Moundsville

OHIO

Summerfield
Station

Jane and her
children were met
near the mouth of the
Little Muskingum by
their guide,
David
Putnam Jr.
They arrived at
Jewett Palmer's
farm before
dawn and
rested for
the entire
long day
before
leaving
for Markey
Station.

Markey
Station

Stafford
Station

At Markey Station Jane and her
family were almost discovered
by members of a posse raised
and lead by their former owner
Soloman Harness when exhausted
members of both groups bedded
down in the same field.

New Martinsville

Palmer
Station

Paden City

Sistersville

At Reno Landing
at the mouth of the
Little Muskingum
escaping slaves got
seperated from
the main party.
They were
recaptured
near Newport.

"OLD"
VIRGINIA

Marietta

Reno
Landing
Station

St Marys

Harness
Plantation
Landing

One night after dark in August of 1843
Jane and her seven children and two other slaves
were met and ferried downstream from the mouth of
Bull Creek by Josephus, "the ferryboat man."

WHERE SHE WENT. The map below is a modern charting of the route taken by the fugitive slave Jane and her seven children during their first five days of travel. There is reason to believe that all eight members of Jane's family made it to Canada, but their journey is documented only as far as the Colins Station at the top of the map. They reached Collins Station by way of Palmer, Markey, Stafford, and Guinea Stations. There is other documentation of these events, some of it available on the following page, and it has been used to generate several written treatments. Henry Burke has written several columns, a monograph, and a historically accurate fictionalized account, titled *The Escape of Jane*. Mr. Burke and Dick Croy have written a historic novel called *The River Jordan*, and Patricia Thomas-Wilson has authored a one-act play that has been produced under the title, *The Escape of Jane*.

JANE'S DOCUMENTATION. The article on the right, which is from the *Marietta Intelligencer* of August 24th of 1843, and the reward poster below are both factual contemporary accounts of the escape of the slave Jane and her seven children from the plantation of Solomon Harness. The article also tells the story of two additional slaves who escaped but became separated from the rest of the party and their conductor and were recaptured. After necessary legal proceedings those poor souls were "delivered to Mr. H. who immediately removed them home."

The reward poster below is computer enhanced. The original, which was taken from a tree in Washington County, Ohio in 1843, was no longer easily readable.

$450 REWARD

RANAWAY from the subscriber, living in *Wood Count* in the state of *Virginia*, **EIGHT** Negro Slaves, to wit: .
JANE, a woman of low stature and very fleshy, and abo fifty years of age, something lame in one leg when walking.
ALFRED, a young man of about *twenty five years* age, spare made, has a remarkable hole in his left jaw, & plays on the Vio Caroline, a heavy built young woman. aged about **23**, copper coloured, n as a scar about one of her eyes, and some freckles. Rachael, a sm spare built woman. quite black, about **22** years of age, with remarka prominent eyes. Augustus, a heavy stout built boy about **16** years old, qu black, and marked on one of his arms under his sleeve with a honey con and plays well on the Violin. Thornton, a boy about **14** years of age, st built, and very bushy headed. Henry, **12** or **13** years old, a handsome rather slender, very black. Fanny, about **8** or **9** years old, has ba burn upon her wrist, leaving a scar differing in color from her skin.
For Alfred I will pay $100; for one and each of the oth named slaves, I will give **$50** each if delivered to me at m residence, in Wood Co. Va. at the mouth of Bull Creek.
S. HARNESS.

REWARD POSTER.

Seven

TOPOGRAPHY

CANAL LOCK

MUSKINGUM RIVER IMPROVEMENT PROJECT, 1836–1841. What can be seen there today has been rebuilt and reduced. In 1841, the lock chambers averaged 35 feet wide and 160 feet long. The doors were made of thick heavy oaken beams. Men walked across the tops of the doors to move from the lock wall to the shore. They were treated with whatever took the place of creosote in the 1830s and pegged together with big iron bolts forged on sight by teams of blacksmiths. Before they were hung, they were caulked and tarred like ship's bottoms. The lock walls were built with the harder grades of sandstone available in the Ohio Valley. They were 14 feet wide at the top, 30 to 40 feet above the water in most places, and expanded six to eight inches per course on the outboard or river side on the way down. From a small skiff on the river, they looked as big as the pyramids. The dams themselves were built in a fashion new to the region. They were covered with a shell of Portland Cement.

THE MUSKINGUM RIVER LINE. Ohio was used to canal building in 1836. They expected the large, and at times, integrated crews of workers that descended on the Muskingum River Valley to build the local sections. Integration then, by the way, meant Irish-American crews working in the same hole with African-American crews, and it was a new practice. It was accepted because there was too much work for the available hands. So the Muskingum River Valley was filled with crews of strangers. When construction was completed, those workers were replaced by lock operators, boat men, and canal users. All the while, a steady portion of the African Americans involved were filtering upstream from dam to dam. When the Portsmouth to Cleveland Canal had been completed nine years earlier, large partisan patrols of "Rangers" had appeared near Portsmouth asking hard questions of every person of color they found and hauling many away to be transported south. Some of those transported were escaped slaves. Others had been free men. Every day there were beatings. Once in a while, someone would be killed. Traffic on the new route simply stopped. Nine years later when the Muskingum River canal extension opened, very few "rangers" showed up and concentrating on the Muskingum Line was simple topography. Other lines did not disappear. Their volume shrank while the Muskingum's grew. North/south rail lines when they came altered the topography again as did Union armies when they started to move. Completion of an east/west railroad line ending at Marietta in 1857 provided more routing opportunities for fugitives and figured heavily in the war to come. But by then the canal extension had been in full operation for 16 years.

Eight

THE MAPS

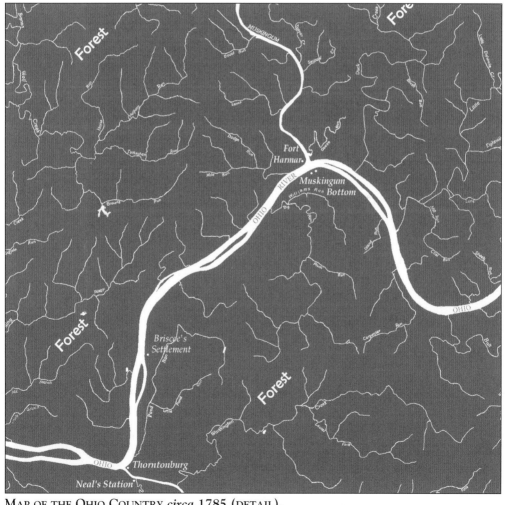

MAP OF THE OHIO COUNTRY *circa* 1785 (DETAIL).

MARIETTA AREA ROUTES AND STATIONS MAP. At full size and in full color, it is possible to read details of incidents occurring along the Underground Routes and at Underground Stations marked on this map. Even as it is here, it reveals the shape of the Underground Network and that is useful. All products a collaboration between Henry Burke and Charles Fogle, the maps appearing in this book are all adapted from U. S. Geological Survey maps or other reliable sources.

All maps used for route illustration in this book are either reworked detail segments of the Marietta Area Map shown on this page or segments of other maps in the Burke/Fogle Map Series. Each map contains as much Underground Railroad information as was known to us at the time of publishing, and they are always subject to revision.

125

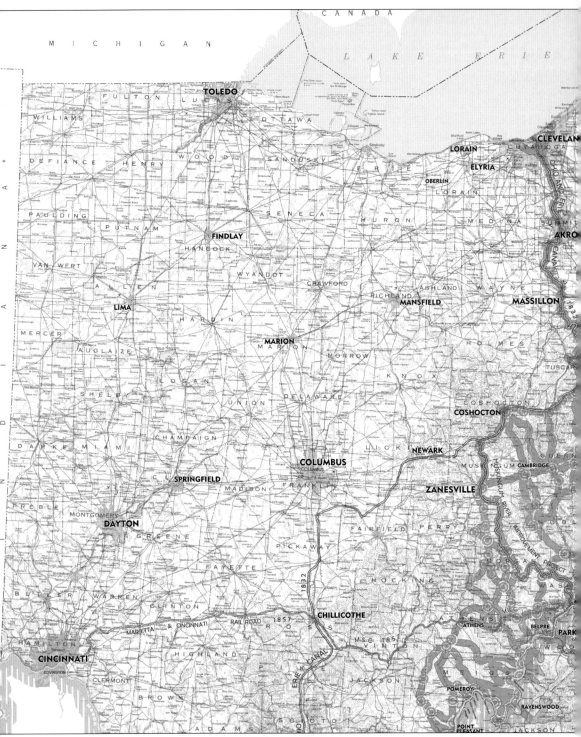

THE MUSKINGUM RIVER LINE MAP. The Muskingum River Line Map includes waterways, turnpikes, canals, and steam railroads with dates where possible, in addition to crossing points, routes, and stationhouses of the Underground Railroad. With this map, it is possible to trace

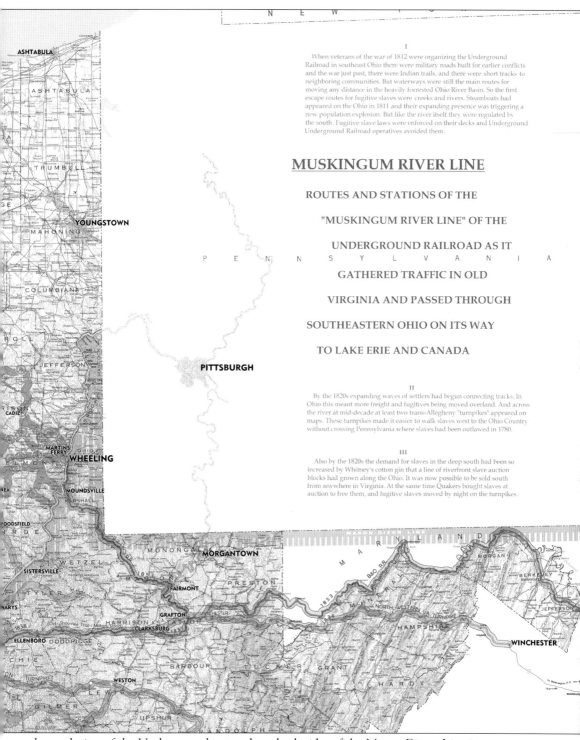

MUSKINGUM RIVER LINE

ROUTES AND STATIONS OF THE

"MUSKINGUM RIVER LINE" OF THE

UNDERGROUND RAILROAD AS IT

GATHERED TRAFFIC IN OLD

VIRGINIA AND PASSED THROUGH

SOUTHEASTERN OHIO ON ITS WAY

TO LAKE ERIE AND CANADA

I

When veterans of the war of 1812 were organizing the Underground Railroad in southeast Ohio there were military roads built for earlier conflicts and the war just past, there were Indian trails, and there were short tracks to neighboring communities. But waterways were still the main routes for moving any distance in the heavily forrested Ohio River Basin. So the first escape routes for fugitive slaves were creeks and rivers. Steamboats had appeared on the Ohio in 1811 and their expanding presence was triggering a new population explosion. But like the river itself they were regulated by the south. Fugitive slave laws were enforced on their decks and Underground Underground Railroad operatives avoided them.

II

By the 1820s expanding waves of settlers had begun connecting tracks. In Ohio this meant more freight and fugitives being moved overland. And across the river at mid-decade at least two trans-Allegheny "turnpikes" appeared on maps. These turnpikes made it easier to walk slaves west to the Ohio Country without crossing Pennsylvania where slaves had been outlawed in 1780.

III

Also by the 1820s the demand for slaves in the deep south had been so increased by Whitney's cotton gin that a line of riverfront slave auction blocks had grown along the Ohio. It was now possible to be sold south from anywhere in Virginia. At the same time Quakers bought slaves at auction to free them, and fugitive slaves moved by night on the turnpikes.

the evolution of the Underground network on both sides of the Mason-Dixon Line in response to changing conditions on the ground.

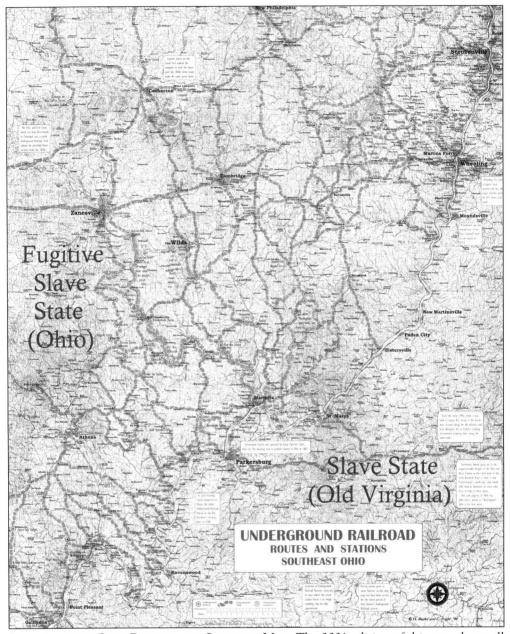

SOUTHEASTERN OHIO ROUTES AND STATIONS MAP. The 2001 edition of this map shows all documented Underground Railroad routes and stations known to the authors in Southeastern Ohio. All maps in this book, unless marked otherwise, are copyrighted work products of a collaboration between H.R. Burke and C.H. Fogle.